CONVENTIONAL WISDOM PLUS

A COMPREHENSIVE GUIDE TO MODERN BRIDGE CONVENTIONS

ADVANCED BIDDING, DEFENDING AND PLAYING CONCEPTS

Copyright © 2008

By

Jean J. Reaves
1213 Ferndale Drive
Auburn, AL 36832
Tel. (334) 887-7150
e-mail cjr1972@bellsouth.net

Jean Reaves is an American Contract Bridge League (ACBL) Certified Teacher and has been featured in an ACBL publication as a Star Teacher. She holds the rank of Silver Lifemaster for masterpoints earned through tournament play at ACBL sanctioned bridge games. Reaves is a graduate of Auburn University, Auburn, AL. She is married to Dr. Carl Reaves, a retired engineer. They have 4 children and 16 grandchildren.

SOURCES AND INSPIRATIONS:

ACBL Bulletin

Marty Bergen
- <u>Points, Schmoints Series: Negative Doubles</u>

Easley Blackwood
- <u>Bidding Slams with Blackwood</u>

Larry Cohen
- <u>The Law of Total Tricks</u>

Audrey Grant
- <u>Commonly Used Bridge Conventions</u>

Edwin B. Kantar
- <u>The Defense of the Hand</u>
- <u>A Treasury of Bridge Tips</u>

Mike Lawrence
- <u>Judgement at Bridge</u>
- <u>Doubles!</u>

William Root
- <u>Modern Bridge Conventions</u>
- <u>How to Play a Bridge Hand</u>
- <u>How to Defend a Bridge Hand</u>

Dorothy Hayden Truscott
- <u>Winning Declarer Play</u>

07 15 10

AuthorHouse™
1663 Liberty Drive, Suite 200
Bloomington, IN 47403
www.authorhouse.com
Phone: 1-800-839-8640

First published by AuthorHouse 4/24/2009

ISBN: 978-1-4389-5668-8 (sc)

Printed in the United States of America
Bloomington, Indiana

This book is printed on acid-free paper.

authorHOUSE®

CONVENTIONAL WISDOM PLUS
For the Advancing Bridge Player

TABLE OF CONTENTS

Contents   **Page No.**

Contents   Page No.

- **Bergen Major Suit Raises**
- **Brozel**
- **DONT**
- **Flannery 2 Diamonds**
- **New Minor Forcing**
- **Ogust**

- **One Notrump Forcing**
- **Responsive Double**
- **Reverse Drury**
- **Two NT Response to A Minor Suit Opening**
- **Weak Jump Shift**

PREVIEW

This manual is a follow-up to <u>Bridge for Beginners</u> which should carry the student from absolute beginner to the intermediate level of expertise. It has recently been updated and revised. Abbreviated reviews are shown on the next few pages.

<u>Conventional Wisdom Plus</u> is a guide to the most widely used bridge conventions in duplicate and party bridge clubs across the United States and in other countries. The discussion of the conventions and numerous other subjects – including defense, playing and bidding – is followed with full hands relating to the topic of study. Bridge tips are included with each hand.

There are entire books written on most of the 10 chapters presented. I have studied many of them in order to incorporate enough information into this book to suffice students up to books slanted toward nationally ranked and/or professional players.

Students in classes or persons studying individually are encouraged to concentrate on each chapter and the related hands incrementally.

Some of the minor details included relate to frequently asked questions from students over the last 25 years of my trying to help others learn this game. It is hoped they will help you avoid some of the mistakes I, and most other players, make on the way to feeling comfortable at the bridge table.

Have fun with this most popular, most wonderful game for a lifetime.

BASIC ONE LEVEL BIDS

A Review: Traditional (Standard) Bids through the Game Level
after Partner Opens on the One Level

Majors

Opener		Responder	Strength	Min. No. of Cards	Forcing Non-Forcing
1 H/S	-	2 H/S	6-9 (10) HCP's	3	Non-forcing
1 H/S	-	1 NT	6-9(10) HCP's	< 3 H/S	Non-forcing
1 H	-	1 S	Unlimited	4	Forcing
1 H/S	-	3 H/S	12+	3	Forcing
1 H/S	-	4 H/S	Less than 10 HCP's	5	Non-forcing
1 H/S	-	2 NT	13-15	< 3 H/S	Forcing
1 H/S	-	3 NT	16-17	< 3 H/S	Non-forcing
1 H/S	-	2 C/D	10+ HCP's	4	Forcing
1 S	-	2 H	10+ HCP's	5	Forcing

Minors

1 C/D	-	2 C/D	6-9 (10) HCP's	5	Non-forcing
1 C/D	-	3 C/D	12-13 HCP's	5	Invitational
1 C/D	-	1 H/S	6-9 (10) HCP's	4	Forcing
1 C/D	-	1 NT	6-9 (10) HCP's	< 4 in major	Non-forcing
1 C/D	-	2 NT	12-14 HCP's	< 4 in major	Forcing
1 C/D	-	3 NT	15-17	< 4 in major	Non-forcing
1 C/D	-	4 H/S	13+	7	Non-forcing
1 C/D	-	5 C/D	13+	5	Non-forcing

1 Notrump
15-17

1 NT	-	2 NT	8-9	Balanced	Invitational
1 NT	-	3 NT	10-14 HCP's	Balanced	Sign Off
1 NT	-	2 C	Reserved for	Stayman	
1 NT	-	2 D/H/S	0+		Sign Off
1 NT	-	3 C/D, 3 H/S	15+	6	Slam Inv.

< less than

Bidding Ranges

Opener	Range	Responder*
13-16 points	Minimum	6-9 (10)
17-18 points	Medium	10-12
19-21 points	Maximum	13+

Opener's Rebids

Hand Value	Options
13-16	A simple rebid of the same suit
	A simple bid of another suit
	A simple raise of responder's suit
	A simple bid of notrump
17-18	A jump in the same suit
	A jump raise in partner's suit
	A reverse bid
18-19	A jump bid in notrump
19-21	A jump shift

Responder's Rebids

Hand Value	Options
10-12	Bid a new suit on 2 or 3 level
	Bid a new suit, then support partner
13-15	Jump in partner's suit
	Bid a new suit, then jump
16-18	Jump in partner's suit
	Name a new suit, then jump
19-21	Jump shift
	Explore for slam

* Responder does not jump shift in a suit on his first response to a one level opening call. The rebid tells the story!

OPENING WITH MARGINAL VALUES

There are various hands that some players will open without the requisite 13 points. Most experts theorize that an early "bid" gets the worm.

Quick Tricks

A = 1 quick trick
AK = 2 quick tricks
AQ = 1 ½ quick tricks
KQ = 1 quick trick
KX = ½ quick trick

The opener needs a minimum of 2 ½ quick tricks. Partner needs 1 ½ quick tricks to respond.

The Rule of Twenty

If the sum of HCP's plus the total number of cards in the two longest suits equals 20, open the bidding:

(S) A K 6 5 2	(H) K J 7 5	(D) 7 5	(C) 9 7
7 + 5 = 12	4 + 4 = 8	0	0
12 + 8 = 20			

The Rule of Fifteen

The Rule of 15 may be used in **fourth** position in order to open a marginal holding.

If the sum of HCP's PLUS the total number of spades held equals 15, open the bidding. Holding several spades is a deterrent to the opponents.

(S) J 9 8 7	(H) A K 10 9 8	(D) K 5	(C) 76
+5	+7	+3	

Open 1 heart.

NON-FORCING, FORCING, INVITATIONAL AND SIGN-OFF BIDS

Non-Forcing Bids

- A single raise of partner's bid (1H-2H)
- A notrump bid at the lowest level possible (1H-1NT)
- A simple bid by opener of a suit <u>lower</u> ranked than his original suit (1D-1H-2C)
- Opener 1 club – responder 1 heart – opener 1 spade

Forcing Bids

- A jump in the same major (1H-3H)
- A new suit bid by responder (1H-1S-2H-3C)
- A jump shift by opener or responder (1C-1D-2H)
- A simple bid by opener of a suit <u>higher</u> ranked than his original suit on the two level (a reverse bid) (1C-1S-2D)
- A bid of a new suit by opener after responder has bid a new suit on the two level (1 spade – 2 hearts – 3 clubs)

Invitational Bids

- Opener 1 spade – responder 2 spades – opener 3 spades
- *Opener 1 spade – responder 2 spades – opener 3 clubs *
- Opener 1NT – responder 2NT
  * The club bid here is a game try. Does my club holding enhance your values? Rebid spades accordingly.

Highly Invitational Bids

- Opener 1 heart – responder 1 spade – opener 3 hearts
- Opener 1 C/D – responder 3 C/D
- Opener 1 heart – responder 1 spade – opener 1NT – responder 3 spades

Sign-Off Bids

- 1NT – 3NT
- 1 H/S – 4H/S
- 1 C/D – 5 C/D

COMPETITIVE BIDDING

BRIDGE IS A BIDDER'S GAME WITH STRONG EMPHASIS ON THE MAJOR SUITS

The takeout double (1) promises 4-4-4-1 support for the unbid suits,

12+ HCP's OR (2) a self-sufficient suit of 5+ cards and 17+ HCP's. The doubler

shows his suit with a rebid.

Responder   On (1) must bid regardless of hand value:

- Under 10 HCP's, a simple bid
- With 10-12, a jump bid
- With 13+, a game bid

On (2) when the doubler bids his suit of 17+, responder:

- Passes with 0-7 HCP's
- Bids game with 8 HCP's and 3-card support
- Rebids his suit with 6+ cards, 10+ HCP's and no support for partner's suit (non-forcing)

The overcall suggests a suit and HCP's worthy of competing for a

contract:

- 5+ cards with 2 of the top honors, 8-16 HCP's
- The change of suit after partner's overcall is NOT forcing.

When using the takeout double or the overcall, the level of bidding and

the vulnerability status should ALWAYS be considered. The doubler assesses

combined hand values and places final contract.

INTRODUCTION

CONVENTIONAL WISDOM PLUS

The preceding lists of Standard American bidding sequences are still "happily" played in many party bridge groups. However, the modern approach by duplicate, computer and tournament players is to intersperse some of them with conventions that more narrowly define hand value. Games and slams can often be reached with less power and some conventions tend to curb intervention by opponents. These new gadgets will, of course, change the meaning of some of the bids shown in the review.

Many conventions currently played by all players – for instance – Gerber and Blackwood – have long been an integral part of bridge. However, some of the conventions discussed in this manual are not known to all players. It is considered unfair and/or unethical to use conventions unfamiliar to opponents without an "announcement" or an "alert". To alert those calls you may use the alert card in the bidding box or simply say "alert" when partner makes an alertable call. The ACBL convention card supplied to duplicate players shows **in red** most of the conventions that must be alerted; it shows in **blue** the responder's call which must be alerted by an announcement. Other conventions may be added in the spaces provided. An opponent may look at your convention card before the bidding has begun or he may ask you **when it is his time to make a call** the meaning of your partner's previous call.

Example

You 1 H/S   Opponent – pass   Partner 2 NT

You – "Alert: that is Jacoby 2NT showing trump support and game forcing values."

The explanation is optional unless the opponent requests one. The next opponent, when it is his turn to bid, may also ask for an explanation. **The one who alerts a call must explain it.**

For partnerships just beginning to employ new conventions, it is suggested that the study of the extensions not covered in class be postponed until the basics of each convention are understood. Use the manual for reference as the need arises – AND – it will!

It is rare for two experienced players (or two "pros") to agree precisely on each and every treatment of a bid; however, you and your partner can make wonderful judgment calls early in your "conventional life" if you concur on each treatment. You have the option of dismissing the use of any and all conventions; but, if you want to go with the flow, some conventions are indispensable.

As suggested earlier, the most important strategy is for you and your partner to be on the same wavelength whether bidding or defending AND whether or not you use a particular convention.

Mr. Kantor states in his book, <u>A Treasury of Bridge Tips</u>, that "a bad agreement is better than no agreement at all"! It's more fun to have "good" agreements.

CHAPTER ONE: NOTRUMP

THE STAYMAN CONVENTION
Non Forcing
(1 NT 15-17 – 2 NT 20-21)

Stayman is one of the most widely used and most beneficial bridge conventions available. The Stayman convention was introduced in a publication by Sam Stayman, a well known bridge enthusiast. His partner, George Rapée, developed the idea. Rapée is listed in the ACBL Hall of Fame for this contribution to bridge.

The **purpose** of Stayman is to enable a partnership to find an **eight-card fit in a major suit after a one- or two-notrump opening bid**. Later we will see how it may be used after a 2-club opening bid. A contract in the majors will usually make more tricks than a notrump contract because of the ruffing values.

The notrump bidder's hand is well defined; however, there are many ramifications of Stayman that opener and responder need to understand because of the variety of hands each is dealt. The most simple and widely used form of Stayman is called Non-Forcing Stayman. The term "non-forcing" means the 2-club bid isn't forcing to game. **Responder's call of two clubs is an artificial bid**. It has nothing to do with the value of the club suit. It is, therefore, a forcing call.

The responder becomes the captain of a partnership after his partner opens in notrump. This is a very important concept that responder must remember! It is up to him to guide the partnership into the best contract.

The responder often has ruffing values and those values are considered in the evaluation of his hand for a suit contract; but, he should be cautious on counting distributional values if there is a possibility of the final contract landing in notrump. Length points may be added in a notrump or suit contract.

The two-club bid by responder after partner opens one notrump is a statement and/or a question. It says "partner, I have at least one four-card major and a minimum of 8 HCP's. If you have four of the same major, I think we should play this hand in a suit."

The Bidding:	Partner	Opponent	You
	1 NT	Pass	2 clubs

Opener's Rebid after Stayman

Opener denies holding a 4-card major by bidding 2 diamonds, an artificial bid. Responder now bids 2 notrump with 8-9 points inviting partner to bid game with 17 HCP's. With 10-15 HCP's responder bids 3 notrump.

The Hands:	Opener	Opponent	Responder (8-9)
	S A K 10		**S** Q 8 7 6
	H Q J 4		**H** K 6
	D A K 10		**D** 9 8 7
	C 10 9 8 7		**C** A 5 4 3
The Bidding:	1 NT	Pass	2 clubs
	2 diamonds		2 NT
	3 NT		

Change the 9 of diamonds to the Queen and responder would bid 3 NT on the above hand. After responder limits his holding on the two level, the opener simply adds his points to those shown by responder.

If NT opener has one 4-card major, he bids 2 of that suit. If that is responder's suit, he raises to 3 with 8 or 9 points. He bids 4 with 10-15 points. If the major was not responder's suit, he once again places the contract according to hand value:

The Hands:	Opener	Opponent	Responder
	S A K 10		**S** Q J 9 8
	H J 10 9 8		**H** A 7 6
	D A K 10		**D** Q 5 4
	C 10 9 8		**C** Q 6 5
The Bidding:	1 NT	Pass	2 clubs
	2 hearts		3 NT

If opener has both 4-card majors he bids hearts first. If hearts is captain's suit, he raises to 3 hearts with 8 or 9 points and bids 4 hearts with 10-15 points. If spades is captain's suit, he responds 2 or 3 notrump, again depending upon hand value. The opening notrump bidder now converts the contract to spades. (The opener knows responder has 4 spades since he used Stayman, then denied having 4 hearts.)

The Hands:	Opener	Opponent	Responder
	S A K 10 9		**S** Q J 8 7
	H J 10 9 8		**H** Q 7
	D A K		**D** Q 9 8 7
	C 10 9 8		**C** A 7 6
The Bidding:	1 NT	Pass	2 clubs
	2 hearts		3 NT
	4 spades		

If the 1 NT opener responds 2 diamonds and partner has 5+ cards in either major, responder bids that major in accordance with HCP's.

The Hands:	Opener	Opponent	Responder
	S A K 10		**S** Q 9 8 7 6
	H Q J 9		**H** K 5
	D A K 5		**D** Q 6 4
	C 10 7 6 5		**C** J 9 8
The Bidding:	1 NT	Pass	2 clubs
	2 diamonds		2 spades (8-9)
	4 spades (maximum)		Pass

From the examples in this section, we can see that remembering how many HCP's are available from partner's responses is very helpful:

Summary

Notrump Opener (15-17)	Responder (8+)
15 – minimum	8 - 9 minimum
16 – medium	10 -14 medium
17 – maximum	15 + slam range

On borderline game-going hands, look for good long suits and/or good "fillers" (10 9 8).

Responder's Rebid after Stayman with Weak Hands

If responder wishes to **sign off in clubs**, he may bid 2 clubs and then 3 clubs. The opener passes. Responder should have a very distributional hand and 6+ cards in the club suit to justify going to the 3 level.

Stayman in Pretense

Responder must always have 5+ cards for his rebid in a suit after using Stayman with one exception i.e., "Stayman in Pretense" which comes up very, very rarely. "Stayman in Pretense" is used on a hand that ALWAYS has a singleton club or a void in clubs and has length in the other three suits. It is used to get partner out of a notrump contract because the hand is so "bleak" ruffing power is needed. Some players call it "garbage Stayman." Responder's holding will be similar to one of the hands shown below:

	Hand #1	Hand #2	Hand #3
Spades	8 7 6 5	J 9 8 7	Q 8 7 6
Hearts	A 8 7 6	7 6 5 4 3	J 7 6 5
Diamonds	9 7 6 5 4	Q 8 7 6	9 8 7 6
Clubs	void	void	4

The Bidding

Opener	Responder
1 NT	2 clubs
2D/H/S	Pass

The above hands will play much better in a suit than in notrump. This might be considered in the same category as a sign-off bid of 2D, 2H or 2S by responder. Ruffing power is most beneficial when one hand is weak and/or contains unusual distribution.

As with all hands, if opponent interferes after partner's 1 NT opening and you have a garbage hand – DO NOT BID – the idea on the hands immediately above is to alleviate partner's distress. If opponents take care of him, you're "off the hook." As in most bidding interferences, a pass should tell partner you have no new information for him.

Responder Bypassing Stayman

If responder has 10-15 HCP's and a 6-card (or longer) major suit, he may bypass Stayman and go directly to game in that suit.

If responder has a very good six-card major and 13-15 points, he may bypass Stayman and bid 3 H/S as a slam invitation.

If responder has a balanced hand with all suits stopped and 15-16 points, he may bid 4 NT (quantitative) or 4 clubs (Gerber) to search for a slam.

If responder has 10-14 points and a fairly balanced hand, there is no need for him to show a good minor suit. He simply adds points and places the contract in 3 notrump. In fact, responder need not bother using Stayman with a 4-3-3-3 hand if he holds good cards in all suits.

A jump to 3 C/D after a 1 NT opening by partner is a slam invitation in that minor. If opener rebids 3 NT, he isn't interested in a slam. If opener's sign-off in 3 NT doesn't squelch responder's appetite for a slam, he may bid 4 clubs or 4 diamonds as a slam try.

If responder has a long suit and less than 8 HCP's, he makes a sign-off bid at the two level in any suit except clubs. The club suit is reserved for Stayman.

This chapter is a lot of information for one convention; but, this is the most indispensable of all conventions with the possible exceptions of Blackwood and the takeout double. Stayman has become so common that most experienced players take for granted that "everybody is doing it."

Handling Interference
after Partner Opens 1 NT

When opponent **doubles** 1 NT, it is for penalty showing an equal number

of HCP's. Stayman is now available for **both** responders.

- Two clubs – Stayman
- 2 D/H/S – **Sign Off**
- 3 D/H/S – 10+ HCP's – **forcing**

When opponent **overcalls, systems are off** and the bidding reverts to

standard.

The Stolen Bid

When opponent overcalls 2 clubs and that was to be your bid (Stayman);

a double called **"Stolen Bid"** is Stayman. Partner responds exactly the same

as if you had bid 2 clubs.

The Cue Bid to Replace Stayman

If opponent bids 2 D/H/S, a cue bid of that suit replaces Stayman.

Responder needs 10+ points since he will be on the 3 level.

Opener	Overcaller	You	Your holding
1 NT	2 diamonds	**3 diamonds**	at least one 4-card major
1 NT	2 hearts	**3 hearts**	4 spades
1 NT	2 spades	**3 spades**	4 hearts

If opener doesn't have the major your cue bid shows, he **must** make some

other call.

The above conventions must be discussed with all partners.

SUMMARY
RESPONSES TO 1 NT (15-17) USING NON-FORCING STAYMAN

Opener	Responder	Meaning
1NT	2C	Stayman. A minimum of 8 HCP's. At least one 4-card major.
1NT	*2C/2H or 2S	5-card suit. Invitational.
1NT	*2C/3C	Sign-off. 6+cards in suit. Less than 8 HCP's.
1NT	*2C/2NT	8-9 balanced HCP's. At least one 4-card major. Invitational.
1NT	*2C/3NT	10-14 balanced HCP's. At least one 4-card major.
1NT	*2C/4NT	15-16 balanced HCP's. At least one 4-card major. Invitation to slam in NT.
1NT	*2C/4C	Gerber. A conventional bid asking for Aces. At least one 4-card major.
1NT	2D/2H/2S	Sign-off. 5+ cards with 0-7 HCP's.
1NT	2NT	8-9 balanced HCP's. Invitational.
1NT	3C/3D	Good 6-card suit. Invitation to slam.
1NT	3H/3S	Good 6-card major. Invitation to slam.
1NT	3NT	10-14 balanced HCP's.
1NT	4C	Gerber. Asking for number of Aces.
1NT	4H/4S	Sign-off. 6+ H/S and less than opening hand.
1NT	4NT	15-16 balanced HCP's. Invitation to slam in NT.

*/ represents first and second bid by responder.

/ represents one of two suits.

- Some of these bids will have a different meaning when we also play Jacoby Transfers. The responder needs 5-card suits when playing Jacoby.

SUMMARY
RESPONSES TO 2NT (20-21) USING NON-FORCING STAYMAN

Opener	Responder	Meaning
2NT	3C	Stayman. A minimum of 4 HCP's and a 4-card major.
2NT	*3C/3H or 3S	5-card suit. Forcing
2NT	*3C/3NT	4-9 points. At least one 4-card major.
2NT	3H or 3S	Slam try. Six-card suit.
2NT	3C/4C	A slam try in clubs. A 4-card major on the side. Forcing.
2NT	4C	Gerber. An Ace-asking bid.
2NT	3C/4D	Slam try in diamonds. A 4-card major suit on the side.
2NT	3NT	4-9 balanced HCP's. Sign-off.
2NT	4H/4S	6-card suit. Sign off.
2NT	4NT	10+ HCP's. Slam invitation in notrump.

*/ represents first and second bid by responder.

/ represents one of two suits.

TIPS

- There is no sign-off bid after a 2NT opener – pass unless you have 4 points.

- You may still use the Stayman Convention with interfering bids by opponents; but, a discussion of this with your partner is necessary.

- The 3NT opening bid is discussed under weak-two and strong-two bids.

- When playing Jacoby Transfers, some of these bids will be changed; but, we need to know both conventions to be able to interchange **partnerships.**

12

Declarer East 4 Hearts
None Vulnerable

STAYMAN
Lead Directing Doubles

North
S A 7
H 9 4 3
D K Q J 10 9
C Q 7 4

West (dealer)
S K 2
H K Q 5
D A 7 6 3
C K J 9 8

East
S Q J 4 3
H A 10 8 7 6
D 4 2
C A 5

South
S 10 9 8 6 5
H J 2
D 8 5
C 10 6 3 2

The Bidding: West 1 NT – North pass – East 2 clubs – South pass – West 2 diamonds – North double – East <u>3</u> hearts – South pass – West 4 hearts – North pass, pass, pass.

The Lead: The 8 of diamonds

Tips: Please note 3 NT will not make. Four hearts should make 10-11 tricks.

<u>If</u> West had responded 2 spades, East would have bid 4 spades never revealing his 5-card heart suit.

East jumped the level of bidding, <u>a forcing to game bid</u>, to ask partner to choose between hearts and notrump.

The double of an artificial bid is lead directing.

Declarer South 3 NT
None Vulnerable

STAYMAN
Bypassing Stayman

North
S Q 10 3 2
H Q 6 5
D K J 8
C K J 10

West
S A 9 8 5 4
H 8 4
D 7 6 5
C 8 5 4

East (dealer)
S --
H K J 10 9
D Q 9 4 3 2
C Q 6 3 2

South (declarer)
S K J 7 6
H A 7 3 2
D A 10
C A 9 7

The Bidding: East pass – South 1 NT – West pass – North 3 NT – East pass, pass, pass.

The Lead: The 5 of spades

Tip: With a balanced hand and stoppers in all suits, it isn't necessary (although not wrong) to use Stayman.

Declarer South 2 Hearts
None Vulnerable

STAYMAN
Lead Directing Double

<u>North</u>
S J 10 6 5
H K Q 6 3
D J 4 3
C 7 4

<u>West</u>
S 8 7 3 2
H J 2
D A 9 7
C 6 5 3 2

<u>East</u>
S Q 9 4
H A 5 4
D 8 5
C K Q J 10 9

<u>South</u> (dealer)
S A K
H 10 9 8 7
D K Q 10 6 2
C A 8

The Bidding: South 1 NT – West pass – North 2 clubs – East double – South 2 hearts – West pass, pass, pass.

The Lead: The 2 of clubs

Tips: The double of all artificial bids is lead directing. The "doubler" must have a pretty good suit because the bidders might decide to play 2 clubs doubled. Back to the bidding. Even though North doesn't have the 8 points required for Stayman, his hand contains two suits with very good fillers. Any time you are within one or two points of the ideal holding, stretch your imagination to see if you can't justify stretching the bidding for a more ideal contract. A pass would not be incorrect.

Other artificial bids that may be doubled for lead direction are cue bids and Gerber.

Declarer North 4 Spades
None Vulnerable

STAYMAN
Watch the Spots

North
S K Q 10 9 8
H 7 4 3
D A J 6
C Q 9

West
S J 3 2
H K Q J 10 9 2
D 10 9
C 6 5

East (dealer)
S 7 6
H 5
D Q 8 7 5 2
C K 7 4 3 2

South (dealer)
S A 5 4
H A 8 6
D K 4 3
C A J 10 8

The Bidding: South 1 NT – West pass – North 2 clubs – East pass – South 2 diamonds, denying a 4-card major – West pass – North <u>3</u> spades, showing a 5-card suit and game-going values – East pass – South <u>4</u> spades, pass, pass, pass.

The Lead: The 5 of hearts

Tips: North counts losers in a suit bid – 2 hearts, 1 club and 1 diamond. When he gains the lead, he draws trumps and works on clubs for a diamond discard.

Declarer discards the 10 of clubs under the Queen, plays the 9 and discards the 8 in order to take 2 finesses for the King of clubs.

East should not cover the Queen of clubs lead from dummy – that is exactly what declarer would love. <u>Cover only if it will promote a trick for your partnership.</u>

Responder doesn't show a suit after partner opens notrump unless it contains a minimum of 5 cards.

Declarer South 3 NT
None Vulnerable

STAYMAN
Defensive Count Signals

North (dealer)
S Q 10 9 5
H K J 10
D J 10 9 4
C A 8

West
S A J 7 6
H 3 2
D K 5
C 9 7 6 3 2

East
S 8 3 2
H Q 9 8 7 6
D 8 3 2
C K 5

South
S K 4
H A 5 4
D A Q 7 6
C Q J 10 4

The Bidding: North pass – East pass – South 1 NT – West pass – North 3 NT – East pass, pass, pass.

The Lead: The 6 of spades

Tips: When responder's hand is balanced, he may bypass Stayman and play the hand in notrump – he is captain and has that option. Sometimes making 9 tricks is easier than making 10 tricks.

Note East's spot cards. A rule in defense is applicable. When third hand holds no card higher than those in dummy, he should give count. High-low shows an even number of cards in the suit led. Low-high shows an odd number. East would discard the 2 of spades on West's opening lead since he holds 3 cards.

Declarer North 4 Spades
None Vulnerable

STAYMAN
Responder's Rebid Tells the Story

North
S A 10 8 7 6
H K 9 8 7
D 5
C A 4 2

West
S K Q 9
H 10 6 5
D 8 7 3 2
C Q 10 3

East (dealer)
S 3 2
H 4 3 2
D K Q 6 4
C 9 8 7 6

South
S J 5 4
H A Q J
D A J 10 9
C K J 5

The Bidding: East pass – South 1 NT – West pass – North 2 clubs – East pass – South 2 diamonds – West pass – North <u>3</u> spades – East pass – South 4 spades – West pass, pass, pass.

The Lead: The 9 of clubs

Tips: As long as responder holds <u>one</u> 4-card major, he may use Stayman. If he holds both majors and one is longer, his <u>rebid</u> denotes the <u>length</u> and <u>strength</u> of his hand. With a minimum of 10 HCP's, he must jump on the rebid to force opener to game. If opener held only 2 spades, his rebid would be 3 notrump.

If playing Jacoby Transfers, the bidding would go: East pass – South 1 NT – West pass – North 2 hearts – South 2 spades – North 4 spades.

Declarer West 2 Hearts
None Vulnerable

STAYMAN
A Sign-off Bid

North (dealer)
S K 5 4 3
H K 10 9
D Q J 3
C K 9 4

West
S 8 2
H J 8 7 6 3 2
D 4 2
C J 10 5

East
S A Q 7 6
H Q 5
D K 8 7 5
C A Q 8

South
S J 10 9
H A 4
D A 10 9 6
C 7 6 3 2

The Bidding: North pass – East 1 NT – South pass – West 2 hearts – North pass, pass, pass.

The Lead: The 3 of spades

Tips: West gives a sign-off bid. This hand will probably make in hearts. If East is the declarer in notrump, he can never get to partner's hand and will have to play those beautiful, unprotected honor cards from his hand. Responder is captain.

If playing Jacoby Transfers, West would bid 2 diamonds transferring the play of the hand to the notrump opener.

Declarer South 3 Spades
None Vulnerable

STAYMAN
When Responder Makes an
Invitational Bid

North
S Q 10 9 8
H K 5
D K 8 7
C J 6 5 4

West (dealer)
S 4 3 2
H A 10 9 8
D Q 9 6 2
C A 10

East
S K 5
H Q J 4 3 2
D 10 5
C 9 7 3 2

South
S A J 7 6
H 7 6
D A J 4 3
C K Q 8

The Bidding: West pass – North pass – East pass – South 1 NT – West pass – North 2 clubs – East pass – South 2 spades – West pass – North 3 spades – East pass, pass, pass.

The Lead: The 2 of diamonds

The Play: Declarer pauses to count losers and to make a plan before playing to the first lead. He should let the diamond lead ride to his hand, taking advantage of a favorable opening lead. He could then lead a small diamond to the King in order to take a finesse for the King of spades. If East covers, South wins and draws the outstanding trumps. When he starts working on the club suit, he plays the high cards from the short side first. This leaves the "long" club in dummy available for a discard.

Tips: Even though responder becomes captain after partner opens 1 NT, he needs help from the opener. He needs to know if opener's hand is minimum, medium or maximum. The opener's pass shows a minimum hand.

IF opener had responded 2 diamonds, North would have bid 2NT. IF South's hand was _medium_, he has to gamble; with a maximum, he would bid game.

Declarer West 2 Diamonds
None Vulnerable

STAYMAN
in Pretense
Garbage Stayman

North
S A 9 6
H 9 7 5 2
D A 5
C Q J 10 4

West (dealer)
S Q 8
H K J 6
D K Q J 2
C A 9 7 6

East
S 7 5 4 2
H Q 10 4 3
D 10 7 6 3
C 3

South
S K J 10 3
H A 8
D 9 8 4
C K 8 5 2

The Bidding: West 1 NT – North pass – East 2 clubs – South pass – West 2 diamonds – North pass, pass, pass. It is always a shock when this bidding sequence happens. It is usually safe because if 1 NT opener doesn't have 4 hearts or 4 spades, he will usually have 4 diamonds. West should make 8 or 9 tricks in diamonds; he could be held to 6 tricks in notrump.

The Lead: Since East is known to be short in clubs, the best defense might be to lead the Ace of diamonds and another diamond to cut down declarer's ability to crossruff. Another option for an opening lead is the Queen of clubs.

Tip: The opportunity to use this "nifty" bid is rare. It goes like this. When responder to a 1 NT opening holds a singleton club (or a void in clubs), his hand will be of more value in a suit contract. Therefore, he bids 2 clubs "pretending" he holds a major suit AND 8 HCP's. He passes any response. It's a fun bid and partner will usually be happy. The current name of this bid is "Garbage Stayman."

Declarer South 3 NT
None Vulnerable

STAYMAN
The Two Notrump Opening Bid
(20-21 HCP's)

North
S K J 9 8
H 6 5
D 9 8 7
C K 8 7 5

West
S 10 7 5 4
H J 10 9
D Q 10 4 3
C A Q

East
S 6 3 2
H K 4 3 2
D 5 2
C 6 4 3 2

South (dealer)
S A Q
H A Q 8 7
D A K J 6
C J 10 9

The Bidding: South 2 NT – West pass – North 3 clubs – East pass – South 3 hearts – West pass – North 3 NT – East pass, pass, pass.

The Lead: The Jack of hearts

Tips: Stayman may also be used after an artificial 2-club opening bid when opener's **rebid** is notrump. The **rebid** shows <u>22</u> HCP's.

You will recall opener's jump bid to 2NT after **partner's response on the one level** shows 18-19 HCP's

- 1 heart – 1 spade (responder) – 2 NT (opener)   18-19 HCP's

- 2 NT opening   20-21 HCP's

- 2 NT rebid after 2 club opening   22-24 HCP's

Declarer South 4 Spades
None Vulnerable

STAYMAN
When Opener Holds
Both 4-card Majors

North
S A 9 5 4
H K 10 6
D A 6 5
C 8 7 2

West
S Q 7 6
H J 9 5
D 8 7 4
C K Q 10 9

East
S 10 8
H 7 3 2
D J 10 3 2
C A 6 5 3

South (dealer)
S K J 3 2
H A Q 8 4
D K Q 9
C J 4

The Bidding: South 1 NT – West pass – North 2 clubs – East pass – South
2 hearts – West pass – North 3 NT – East pass – South 4 spades – West pass,
pass, pass.

The Lead: The King of clubs

Tip: When responder bids 2 clubs after partner opens 1 NT (always Stayman),
his rebid denotes strength and shape. North responded 3 NT, denying having
4 hearts – BUT – game-going values. South then placed the contract in
4 spades; if North doesn't have 4 hearts, he has 4 spades.

Declarer South 6 Hearts
None Vulnerable

STAYMAN
Use Gerber after First and Last Notrump

North
S K 3 2
H A J 5 2
D A Q J 7
C K J

West
S Q J 9
H 9 8
D 10 9 5 2
C 7 6 4 3

East
S 10 8 5 4
H Q 10 7
D 8 6 4
C 9 8 5

South (dealer)
S A 7 6
H K 6 4 3
D K 3
C A Q 10 2

The Bidding: South 1 NT – West pass – North 2 clubs – East pass – South 2 hearts – West pass – North 4 clubs – East pass – South 4 spades, showing 2 Aces – West pass – North 6 hearts – East pass, pass, pass.

The Lead: The Queen of spades

The Play: South has only a 50-50 chance of the heart finesse working. If it doesn't work, he will lose a spade trick and be defeated. The odds are more in his favor to cash the AK of hearts and then play the top diamonds and discard spades. Even if East trumps the third diamond, he gets only 1 trick.

Tips: Any time you hold 15-16 HCP's and partner opens 1 NT, think slam!

North first used Stayman to find a 4-4 fit in hearts. Once the trump suit is set, responder's rebid denotes his strength.

The 4 club bid is Gerber, an Ace-asking bid.

Declarer North 4 Hearts
N-S Vulnerable

STAYMAN
When Partner Doubles a NT Opening

North
S K 10 6 4
H A 5 3 2
D A 10 9
C K J

West (dealer)
S A J
H K Q
D Q J 5 4 2
C Q 5 4 3

East
S 5 3 2
H 7 6 4
D 8 6 3
C 8 7 6 2

South
S Q 9 8 7
H J 10 9 8
D K 7
C A 10 9

The Bidding: West 1 NT – North double – East pass – South 2 clubs – West pass – North 2 hearts – East pass – South 4 hearts – West pass, pass, pass.

The Lead: The top of nothing

The Play: All of the outstanding HCP's must be with West; therefore, declarer plays for all of them to be there.

Tip: When partner doubles a 1 NT opening bid, he has a NT opening hand or more. Therefore, systems are on i.e., Stayman or Jacoby. The doubler's partner responds exactly as if partner opened 1 NT.

Declarer West 2 Spades
None Vulnerable

STAYMAN
After a 1 NT Opening
by Opponent

North (dealer)
S K 10 6 4
H A 8 3 2
D A 10 8
C K J

West
S 9 7 5 3 2
H K 10
D 5 4 2
C 5 4 3

East
S A Q J
H Q J
D Q J 9 6 3
C Q 10 9

South
S 8
H 9 7 6 5 4
D K 7
C A 8 7 6 2

The Bidding: North 1 NT – East Double – South pass – West 2 spades – North pass, pass, pass.

The Lead: The Ace of hearts

The Play: Declarer wins the second heart lead and plays the Queen of diamonds. South should play second hand high and play another diamond hoping to use his singleton trump.

Tips: When partner doubles a 1 NT opening bid, systems are on as if he had opened 1 NT in first position.

West signed off in two spades since his hand is too weak to help defeat 1 NT.

THE GAMBLING 3 NT

The gambling 3 NT opening bid is based on a 7-card, solid minor suit.
The hand doesn't have an outside Ace and very few other honor cards. It is
preemptive; yet it makes pretty often. If it doesn't, the opponents will usually
have "tickets" for a major suit contract.

Examples

	Hand #1	**Hand #2**
S	10 2	J 10
H	J 5	9 8
D	10 9	A K Q 8 7 6 2
C	A K Q 8 7 6 2	J 6
The bid: 3	NT	3 NT

If partner cannot "stand" the contract, he pulls the bid to 4 clubs. If clubs
is opener's suit, he passes. If opener's long suit is diamonds, he pulls the
contract to diamonds and his partner passes.

The defense is different from other notrump contracts. Lead an Ace, see
dummy and partner's "attitude". If you get a card below the 6, try another Ace or
another suit until you hit upon the one most likely to defeat the contract.

If right-hand opponent doubles immediately after a gambling 3 NT bid,
responder may redouble to play 3 NT or **redouble asking partner to pull the
contract to 4 of the minor**. Partners must agree on which to use. Prefer the
latter in this class.

Declarer North 4 Diamonds

None Vulnerable

The Gambling 3 NT

North (dealer)
S 9 6
H 5 4
D A K Q 10 9 8 7
C Q 6

West
S 10 7 3 2
H A K
D 3 2
C A 5 4 3 2

East
S A K 5
H Q 7 6 3 2
D 5 4
C K 9 7

South
S Q J 8 4
H J 10 9 8
D J 6
C J 10 8

The Bidding: North 3 NT – East pass – South 4 clubs – West pass – North 4 diamonds – East pass, pass, pass.

The Lead: The Ace of spades

The Play: West plays the 2. East switches to the 3 of hearts. West wins, plays the Ace, cashes the Ace of clubs and returns a spade.

Tips: The gambler's partner needs quick tricks and/or early "stoppers" to let the 3 NT bid stand.

　　　The defense needs to take all tricks available before relinquishing the lead.

THE JACOBY TRANSFER
Opening Ranges of 15-17 (1 NT) 20-21 (2 NT)

There are wonderful aids to help us get into wonderful contracts after partner opens 1 NT. While studying the Stayman Convention we learned that responder could help partner find a major suit contract and that the big hand could usually be concealed. Jacoby also allows us to get into better playing contracts.

There is an obvious difference as to when responder uses Jacoby – as opposed to Stayman; his **major must contain a minimum of 5 cards**. The pointcount for a transfer response may range from 0 up! The idea on weak hands is to get partner out of a notrump contract which often plays poorly when responder is broke or when he holds "wild" distribution.

The Jacoby Transfer originated in Sweden and was made popular in the United States by Oswald Jacoby. Either he or his son, both of whom are famous in the bridge world, introduced Jacoby 2 NT (another convention) to help partnerships reach a slam contract with less HCP's by taking advantage of distribution. It isn't related to the Jacoby Transfer; Jacoby 2NT is used after partner opens a major suit. It will be discussed later.

Responder may use the transfer when he holds one 5-card major suit, two 5-card majors or one 5-card major and one 5-card minor. If responder holds one 5-card major and one 5-card minor, he transfers to the major and then **bids** his minor suit. 1NT – 2 hearts (transfer) – 2 spades (acceptance) – **3 clubs** (responder's second suit). If responder holds 5/5 (or more) in the majors, he transfers to spades and then bids hearts. As stated, the purpose of the transfer is to allow the stronger hand – most often held by the notrump opener – to stay concealed. It is also advantageous for the lead to come into declarer's hand.

To transfer, the responder bids the suit immediately below the major he holds.

(1 NT (opener) – 2 diamonds (you) – 2 hearts (opener)) OR
(1 NT – 2 hearts –2 spades)

The responder's rebid will further describe his hand value.

Listed below are examples of hands a responder may hold and how he responds after his partner opens 1 NT.

Hand # 1

Opener's Bid	Responder Holds	Responder's Call
1 NT	S Q 10 8 6 5 H 10 9 D J 9 5 4 C 7 6	2 hearts
2 spades		pass

The transfer and then a pass on Hand # 1 is equivalent to the sign-off bid when using Stayman. The hand above will make 2 spades more often than it will make a 1 NT contract. Ruffing power really helps with a weak hand.

Hand # 2

Opener's Bid	Responder Holds	Responder's Call
1 NT	S 10 8 5 H K J 10 9 8 D A K 7 C 3 2	2 diamonds
2 hearts		3 notrump
Pass with only 2 hearts Bid 4 hearts with 3+		

Hand # 3

Opener's Bid	Responder Holds	Responder's Call
1 NT	**S** Q J 10 9 8 6	2 hearts
	H 8 7 6	
	D Q 4	
	C Q 2	
2 spades		3 spades
		(invitational)
Pass with 15-16; bid		
4 spades with 16-17*		

On hand # 3, note the responder raised the suit he transferred. **This shows a minimum of 6 cards**. Responder's 3-spade bid is invitational. It shows 8-9 points. Dummy points may be added since the contract should be in a suit with an 8-card trump suit. On the above hand (and all hands) count the value of the two Queens only. Do NOT include values for doubletons containing an honor.

Hand # 4

Responder is 5/5 in the majors

Opener's Bid	Responder Holds	Responder's Call
1 NT	**S** K J 9 8 2	2 hearts
	H Q J 10 9 8	
	D 4	
	C 9 2	
2 spades		4 hearts
4 spades or Pass		

Counting distributional values, responder jumps to 4 hearts. The opener takes his choice. If responder holds 8-9 points he stays on the 3 level (hearts) to give opener a choice.

_____

* Consider hand structure.

Hand # 5

Opener's Bid	Responder Holds	Responder's Call
1 NT	**S** 6	2 diamonds
	H A Q J 9 8 4 3	
	D K 5	
	C K 10 4	
2 hearts		6 hearts

There is more than one way responder might handle Hand # 5: by using Jacoby, by direct bidding (1 NT – 6 hearts), by using Gerber or by responding 3 hearts, showing 6+ cards and slam invitational values.

There is another important consideration on this particular hand – note responder's holding – this time any lead coming into his hand would be beneficial to declarer. He has the prerogative to make himself declarer.

Signing Off in a Minor Suit
when Playing Jacoby Transfer

The responder to a 1NT opening bid is also dealt distributional hands with long minor suits which might prove difficult to play in notrump. Having used every suit except spades to move openers out of notrump contracts, it was decided responder needed a place to run when he held a long minor suit and an otherwise uneventful hand.

These hands may be assigned to a **minor suit contract** by a response of 2 spades to a 1NT opening bid. The opener now bids 3 clubs. If clubs is responder's long minor, he passes. If his suit is diamonds, he converts to diamonds and the notrump opener passes.

Hand # 6

Opener's Bid	Responder Holds	Responder's Call
1 NT	**S** 8 7 6 **H** J 8 5 **D** Q **C** Q 10 9 8 7 6	2 spades
3 clubs		Pass

Hand # 7

Opener's Bid	Responder Holds	Responder's Call
1 NT	**S** Q **H** 9 8 4 **D** Q 9 7 6 5 4 3 **C** 8 6	2 spades
3 clubs Pass		3 diamonds

The **responder needs 6+ cards** in his suit to convert to a 3-level contract.

The transfer to a minor isn't used after a 2NT opening because the contract

would be at a level too high to justify the bid. If responder is interested in a game

contract or a slam, he would immediately jump to 3 C/D on the above hand.

Summary
After Partner Opens 1 NT

1 NT
- 2 diamonds transfer to hearts
- 2 hearts transfer to spades
- 2 spades transfer to clubs

Jacoby after Partner Opens 2NT

The Jacoby Transfer is equally effective after partner opens 2 NT (20-21

HCP's), rebids 2 NT after a 2-club opening bid (22-24 HCP's) or rebids 3 NT

(25+ HCP's). See next chapter.

Summary
Notrump Rebids after a Two-Club Opening

Partner	Responder
• 2 clubs	• 2 any suit
• 2 NT (rebid)	• 3 NT shows 4+ HCP's • 3 clubs, Stayman • 3 diamonds, transfer to hearts • 3 hearts, transfer to spades
• 3 NT (rebid)	• 4 clubs, slam try in clubs • 4 diamonds, transfer to hearts • 4 hearts, transfer to spades • 4 NT, quantitative • pass unless you are interested in a major suit contract or a slam

Hand # 8

Opener's Bid	Responder Holds	Responder's Call
2 clubs	**S** J 9 6 5 4 3 **H** 9 8 **D** K 10 9 **C** 5 4	2 diamonds
2 notrump		3 hearts
3 spades		4 spades

A two-club opening call followed by two notrump shows 22-24 HCP's.

Therefore, responder needs only 3-4 HCP's to bid game on Hand # 8.

Hand # 9

Opener's Bid	Responder Holds	Responder's Call
2 clubs	**S** J 5 **H** 10 9 8 7 6 5 **D** Q 5 4 **C** 8 7	2 diamonds
3 NT (rebid)		4 diamonds
4 hearts		Pass

A two club opening followed by a 3NT call shows 25+ HCP's.

34

Summary
Handling Interference after Partner Opens Notrump

When an opponent **doubles** after partner opens 1 NT, **all systems are on**

since the level of the bidding hasn't changed! The double of 1 NT is for penalty.

- * Redouble = S.O.S
- 2 clubs = Stayman (regular or Garbage)
- 2 D/H/S = transfer
- 3 C/D = slam invitation
- 3 H/S = slam invitation
- 4 C = Gerber
- 4 NT = Quantitative

* A redouble by responder after opponent's penalty double asks partner
to escape to his best suit.

When an opponent **overcalls** after partner opens 1NT all **systems are off**

and the bidding reverts to standard bidding, i.e.:

- A two-level call shows 5+ cards and is nonforcing.
- A 3-level call shows 5+ cards, 10+ HCP's. Forcing.
- A game bid is to play. It shows a very good 5-card suit
  (preferably 6) and 10+ HCP's.

Stolen Bid

If right-hand opponent overcalls 2 clubs, a double, called **"Stolen Bid"** is

used as **Stayman**. In other words, the opponent "stole" the bid you were

planning to make. The NT opener makes the same response he would have

made without the 2-club overcall by opponent. If the responder's 2 club

(Stayman) response is doubled, (lead directing) opener may:

- Make his normal rebid
- Pass or redouble with 4 or 5 good clubs

The Cue Bid to Replace Stayman

A **cue bid** of right-hand opponent's suit – diamonds, hearts or spades –

is used as **Stayman**. It shows at least one 4-card major.

Partner	Opponent	You
1 NT	2 D/H/S	3 D/H/S

- The cue bid says nothing about the suit bid.
- If responder has stoppers in opponent's suit, he should bid 2/3 NT or double for penalty. A notrump raise doesn't necessarily show stoppers in any suit other than the opponent's.

Stayman NOT Jacoby

If responder holds a 5/4 hand in the majors, he uses Stayman NOT

Jacoby.

Jacoby NOT Stayman

If responder is 6/4 in the majors, he uses Jacoby NOT Stayman. Partner

will have at least two cards in the suit since one doesn't open NT with a

singleton.

36

Summary
The Notrump Opening Bid

Opener	Responder
• 1 NT	2 NT (8-9 HCP's)
• 1 NT	3 NT (10-14 HCP's)
• 1 NT	2 clubs, Stayman
• 1 NT	3 clubs / diamonds / hearts or spades, slam invitation
• 1 NT/2 D,H,S	Transfer
• 1 NT	4 clubs, Gerber
• 1 NT	4 NT, quantitative All game bids are to play unless Texas Transfers are used.

Texas Transfer

The Texas Transfer is made at the **4 level**:

- 1 NT – 4 diamonds transfer to hearts
- 1 NT – 4 hearts transfer to spades

Texas shows a weaker more distributional type of hand and 6+ cards in the suit transferred. Suggestion: To decrease mental fatigue, save this bid until you feel comfortable with low-level transfers. A regular transfer can get you to the same place most of the time.

With Interference

- Systems on after a double
- Systems off after an overcall (bidding reverts to standard)

Declarer North 2 Spades
None Vulnerable

The Jacoby Transfer
Sign-off in a Major

North (dealer)
S A K 2
H A J 5
D K 6 7
C 10 9 8 4

West
S 3
H 4 3 2
D A 4 3 2
C A K 5 3 2

East
S J 9 7 4
H K Q 7 6
D Q 10 8
C Q J

South
S Q 10 8 6 5
H 10 9 8
D J 9 5
C 7 6

The Bidding: North 1 NT – East pass – South 2 hearts – West pass – North 2 spades – East pass, pass, pass.

The Lead: The King of hearts

The Play: Win the Ace of hearts. Play the AK of spades and finesse East for the Jack/9. Play the 10 of hearts and allow East to take his Queen and play to you. Meanwhile, West's first 2 discards are the 5-3 of clubs. High-low says I like!

Tip: South knows North may hold only 2 spades; but, with only 3 HCP's, a suit bid will play much better than NT.

Declarer South 4 Hearts
None Vulnerable

The Jacoby Transfer

North
S 10 8 5
H K J 10 9 8 7
D A K
C 3 2

West
S 9 7 6
H Q 2
D Q 5 4 3
C A 8 7 6

East (dealer)
S Q 3 2
H 5 4 3
D J 8 7 6
C J 10 9

South
S A K J 4
H A 6
D 10 9 2
C K Q 5 4

The Bidding: East pass – South 1 NT – West pass – North 2 diamonds – East pass – South 2 hearts – West pass – North 4 hearts – East pass, pass, pass.

The Lead: The 9 of spades or a small heart.

The Play: Win the lead, draw trumps (probably straight) – finesse East for the Queen of spades. Play a small club toward the KQ.

Tip: The player using Jacoby <u>never</u> <u>rebids</u> the suit transferred unless he holds 6 cards in the suit. With 10+ he bids game in the 6/2 fit in the major. With only 5 cards, he bids 3NT giving opener a choice.

Declarer North 3 Diamonds
None Vulnerable

The Jacoby Transfer
Sign-off in a Minor

North
S 7
H 5 4
D K Q 8 7 6 5 2
C 8 7 6

West
S 5 4 3
H Q J 10 9 6
D A 4
C A 10 9

East
S Q J 10 8 6 2
H 3 2
D J
C Q J 5 4

South (dealer)
S A K 9
H A K 8 7
D 10 9 3
C K 3 2

The Bidding: South 1 NT – West pass – North 2 spades – East pass – South 3 clubs – West pass – North 3 diamonds – East pass, pass, pass.

The Lead: The Queen of spades

The Play: Win the spade lead, play another spade and discard a club. Play the 10 of diamonds. If West doesn't play the Ace, insert the King or Queen and then play the other honor – unblock the diamond suit, throw the 9 under the Queen and put the losers on the long diamonds.

Tip: To transfer to a minor, responder bids 2 spades. If opener bids the minor held by responder, responder passes. If he holds the other minor, he bids it and opener passes.

Declarer South 4 Spades
None Vulnerable

The Jacoby Transfer
The Two Notrump Opening Bid

North
S K J 9 8 6 4
H 6 5
D 9 8
C K 8 7

West
S 10 7 5
H J 10 9
D Q 10 7 4 3
C A Q

East
S 3 2
H K 4 3 2
D 5 2
C 6 5 4 3 2

South (dealer)
S A Q
H A Q 8 7
D A K J 6
C J 10 9

The Bidding: South 2 NT – West pass – North 3 hearts – East pass – South 3 spades – West pass – North 4 spades – East pass, pass, pass.

The Lead: The Jack of hearts

The Play: East should not play the King on partner's Jack – the lead of the Jack denies holding the Queen. Win the heart lead with the Queen – play the AQ of spades – then the Ace of hearts and trump a heart – draw outstanding trumps. Go to closed hand and lead the Jack of clubs.

Tip: When North raised spades, he showed a 6-card suit.

Declarer South 4 NT
None Vulnerable

The Jacoby Transfer
A Slam Try after Jacoby

North
S K J 10 7 3
H K J 5
D A 10 9
C K 10

West
S Q 4
H A 10 9
D 5 4 2
C A 8 6 5 4

East
S 9 8 5 2
H 8 7 6 4
D 7 6
C 9 7 2

South (dealer)
S A 6
H Q 3 2
D K Q J 8 3
C Q J 3

The Bidding: South 1 NT – West pass – North 2 hearts – East pass – South 2 spades – West pass – North 4 NT – East pass, pass, pass.

The Lead: The 5 of clubs

The Play: Declarer wins the King of clubs and leads a small spade to the Ace. He counts his winners while planning his play – 2 spades and 5 diamonds. He develops the spade suit for discards from the closed hand and plays the diamond suit for discards in dummy.

Tips: North's 4 NT call is a quantitative bid. He asked South to bid slam with a maximum opening. Since South's hand is minimum in HCP's and he holds only 2 spades, he elected to play in 4 NT.

Gerber is used after a notrump opening to ask for the number of Aces held **regardless of the other suits shown.**

Declarer South 2 Spades
None Vulnerable

The Jacoby Transfer
Signing Off in a Major

North
S A Q 10 8 6
H 8 7 2
D 4 3
C 10 9 8

West
S 9
H Q 10 6 4 3
D J 10 9 2
C K J 5

East
S K 7 4 2
H A 9
D K 8 5
C Q 7 3 2

South (dealer)
S J 5 3
H K J 5
D A Q 7 6
C A 6 4

The Bidding: South 1 NT – West pass – North 2 hearts – East pass – South 2 spades – West pass – North pass, pass, pass.

The Lead: The Jack of diamonds

The Play: Win the diamond Queen and play a small spade to the 10. East may try the 2 of clubs, leading through strength up to weakness on the board.

Tips: Almost every convention requires us to make changes in the "way it used to be." If we play transfers, we give up the way we made a sign-off bid using the Stayman Convention. On the above hand, using Stayman, North's 2 spade bid would be a sign-off call and he would play the hand.

Declarer South 4 Spades
None Vulnerable

The Jacoby Transfer
Holding both Majors

North
S A 10 9 6 4
H K Q J 10 9
D 6 2
C 5

West
S 8 5 3
H 7 4
D K Q J 4
C A 6 4 3

East
S 7
H 6 5 2
D 10 7 5 3
C Q J 9 7 2

South (dealer)
S K Q J 2
H A 8 3
D A 9 8
C K 10 8

The Bidding: South 1 NT – West pass – North 2 hearts – East pass – South 2 spades – West pass – North 4 hearts – East pass – South 4 spades – West pass, pass, pass.

The Lead: The King of diamonds

The Play: Win the diamond lead, draw trumps, run the heart suit discarding the losing diamond and one club. Lead the singleton club toward the King.

Tip: When responder holds two 5-card majors, he transfers to spades and then bids hearts. He bids 3 hearts with 8-9 points. He bids 4 hearts with 10-14 points.

Declarer South 4 Spades
None Vulnerable

The Jacoby Transfer

North
S A Q 9 5 4
H J 10
D Q J 10
C K 5 4

West
S 3
H K 9 7 6 5
D 7 6 4 2
C J 8 3

East
S K J 6 2
H 8 4 3 2
D 5 3
C Q 7 6

South (dealer)
S 10 8 7
H A Q
D A K 9 8
C A 10 9 2

The Bidding: South 1 NT – West pass – North 2 hearts – East pass – South 2 spades – North 3 NT – East pass – South 4 spades – West pass, pass, pass.

The Lead: The 7 of diamonds (top of nothing)

The Play: South counts losers = 2 clubs, 1 heart and 4 spades. He might win the diamond in dummy, play a small club to the Ace and then the 10 of spades and let it ride. (If the finesse works, South will still be in his hand to repeat the finesse.) East wins and plays through strength and up to the weakest suit, hearts, in dummy.

Tip: DECLARER / ARCH = **A**nalyze the lead, **R**eview the bidding and **C**ount losers before deciding "**H**ow" to play the hand.

Declarer South 4 Hearts
None Vulnerable

The Jacoby Transfer

North
S 3
H 10 9 7 6 5 4 2
D A K
C 7 5 2

West
S K 9 7 6
H 8
D Q J 10 3
C Q 10 9 8

East
S J 10 8 5 2
H K 3
D 9 5 4
C A 6 3

South (dealer)
S A Q 4
H A Q J
D 8 7 6 2
C K J 4

The Bidding: South 1 NT – West pass – North 2 diamonds – East pass – South 2 hearts – West pass – North 4 hearts – East pass, pass, pass.

The Lead: The Queen of diamonds

The Play: Declarer wins two diamond tricks, plays 3 rounds of trumps (to unblock the suit), trumps a diamond and plays a small club toward the King of clubs. With 10 trumps, one would hope the King would fall under the Ace. It doesn't here. When trumps and winners are unblocked, he plays a small club toward the King, goes to dummy and discards losers.

Tips: This hand would probably be defeated in a notrump contract because of the limited transportation between the two hands. With 7 cards in a major suit, place the contract where it has the best chance for success. You know partner has at least 2 hearts – he opened 1 NT!

CAPPELLETTI CONVENTION
To Compete after Opponent Opens 1 NT

Cappelletti, whom I played against the first time my partner, Bobbie Shaw, and I played his convention, developed this system to compete in the bidding after an opponent opens 1 NT. You will recall (Standard American) interference with a double shows 15+ HCP's. An overcaller's hand may contain less HCP's but good distribution. The double will retain its same meaning when playing Cappelletti. The "overcalls" change dramatically, as follows:

Cappelletti

Opponent	You	Partner
1 NT	* 2 clubs	2 diamonds
pass	** 2 H/S	pass

*A relay to diamonds shows a one-suited hand.
**You have a good heart or spade suit.

Opponent	You	Partner
1 NT	2 clubs	2 diamonds
	pass	

Diamonds is your suit.

Opponent	You
1 NT	3 clubs

Clubs is your suit. This is the place you would have landed had you gone through the relay.

Opponent	You	Partner
1 NT	2 diamonds	2 hearts or 2 spades

The bid of 2 diamonds shows both majors.

Opponent	You	Partner
1 NT	2 hearts or spades	• Give support • Bid 2NT to find the minor

The bid of 2 hearts or spades shows that suit <u>and</u> an unspecified minor.

Opponent	You	Partner
1 NT	2 NT	Bid best minor

The bid of 2 NT shows both minors.

You will usually pass unless you think there are values for game.

Summary Cappelletti			
Opponent	**You**	**Your Holding**	**Partner's Response**
1 NT Rebid	2 clubs 2 hearts or 2 spades	one suited	2 diamonds Pass
1 NT Rebid	2 clubs pass	diamonds	2 diamonds
1 NT	<u>3</u> clubs	clubs	pass
1 NT Rebid	2 diamonds pass	hearts (and) spades	bid best major
1 NT	2 hearts **OR** 2 spades	that major and an unspecified minor	3 hearts or 3pades 2 NT to ask for minor
1 NT Rebid	2 NT pass	both minors	bid best of two minors

With any interference, Cappelletti is off and bidding reverts to standard.

See additional conventions that may be used to compete for a contract after opponents open 1 NT under "Other Popular Conventions," page 217.

CHAPTER TWO: THE STRONG ARTIFICIAL 2 CLUB OPENING BID

The two-club opening bid is strong, artificial and forcing. The bid goes hand-in-hand with the weak-two bid of 2 diamonds, 2 hearts and 2 spades which is discussed under preempts. One cannot be used without the other.

Mr. William Root states in his outstanding book, <u>Commonsense Bidding</u>, that the artificial bid of 2 clubs is far superior to traditional strong-two bids. That must be true because most modern-day bridge players are using the bid and most modern authors rarely mention the original style.

The 2-club bid shows one of the two types of hands described below.

- 22+ HCP's with balanced distribution
- 22+ HCP's with a strong suit of 5+ cards

The opener reveals which type of hand he holds on his rebid. This is a forcing bid. **The responder may not pass until game is reached unless he gives a negative 2 diamond response AND the opener rebids the same suit.**

Responder may pass: 2 clubs – 2 diamonds – **2 spades** – 3 clubs – **3 spades** (opener bid same suit)

May not pass: 2 clubs – 2 diamonds – **2 spades** – 3 clubs – **3 hearts** (opener changes suit)

A 2-club opening bid will be similar to one of the following:

S A K J 10 9	**S** A K Q 10 9 8 7
H A 5	**H** --
D Q J 9 8	**D** K Q J 9
C A K	**C** A K

The responder's first call shows a hand that is one of the 3 types shown below:

- Two diamonds shows 7 or less HCP's; and/or,
  2 diamonds may show 8+ lacking the requisite
  5-card suit for a positive bid (waiting).

- Two notrump shows 8+ scattered HCP's. It may
  not show a stopper in every suit.

- Two hearts, 2 spades, 3 clubs or 3 diamonds
  shows 8+ HCP's and a 5-card suit with 2 honors.

Putting It Together on the Rebids after a 2 Club Opening Bid

Opener	Responder
2 clubs	2 diamonds (7 or less HCP's or waiting)
2 spades (real suit 5+cards)	*2 notrump (denies 3 spades)
3 hearts	4 hearts (shows preference for hearts)
pass	
2 clubs	2 hearts (8+ HCP's, 5 hearts)
2 spades	3 hearts (6 hearts, denies 3-card spade suit)
4 hearts	4 NT (Blackwood)
5 spades (3 Aces)	6 hearts
pass	
2 clubs	2 diamonds (negative or waiting)
**2 NT (22-24) (not forcing)	3 clubs (Stayman)
	4 clubs (Gerber)
	3 NT to play
	4 NT quantitative slam try
	4 D/H transfer
2 clubs	2 diamonds
3 NT (25-26)	4 clubs, slam try in clubs
	4 D/H transfer
2 clubs	2 diamonds
4 NT (27+)	Bid 6 NT with 5+ HCP's

*If responder holds 0-4 HCP's, he uses the cheapest minor to show a second negative. (2 clubs – 2 diamonds – 2 hearts – 3 clubs)

**Just as an opening bid of 2NT isn't forcing, the 2NT rebid by the 2 club opener isn't forcing. With 0-3 HCP's, pass.

CHAPTER THREE: SLAM BIDDING

Making a slam can bring one a wonderful sense of accomplishment and enjoyment and it isn't much more difficult than bidding and making any other contract. It just takes a few more HCP's, a little more investigating, and a knack for **trump management and side-suit development**.

Some experts put even more emphasis on the trick-taking potential of a hand than on HCP's – i. e. long, solid suits headed by Aces and Kings to provide first- and second-round controls in every suit:

EXAMPLES

Typical Opening	Trick Taking Opening
S A K J 9 8 6	**S** A K Q J 10 9 8
H Q 2	**H** --
D A J 10	**D** A 10
C A K	**C** K Q J
5 losers	2 losers

Guidelines for Bidding a Slam

- Small slam   12 tricks   33 points
- Grand slam   13 tricks   37 points
- Minimum of 8 cards in the trump suit

Who Goes First?

When it is decided to move toward a slam, either partner may initiate

proceedings by one of three methods:

- By direct bidding
- By cue bidding controls
- By employing the Gerber or Blackwood Convention

The one who goes should not hold two worthless cards in an unbid suit.

DIRECT BIDDING

Direct Bidding is the most simple and quickest way to get to slam. The

partnership simply adds points together. For instance, partner opens 1 NT and

you also have a NT opening. (15 + 17 = 32 – close enough!)

North	South
S A Q J 4	S K 5 3
H K 10 9 8	H A J 10
D A 10 9	D K 8 5
C K 5	C A Q
The Bidding	
1 NT	6 NT

North	South
S A K 10 9 8	S Q J 6 4
H Q J 5	H --
D J 10 9 8	D A Q 5 2
C A Q	C K J 10 9 8
The Bidding	
1 spade	6 spades

Occasionally it takes more bidding, but the contract is reached without the

use of Gerber or Blackwood.

CUE BIDDING TO SLAM

The cue bid in bridge is used in several areas of investigation and/or declaration. In fact, one of the strongest bids partner can make after an opposing bid is to name the same suit as the opponent bid. It is used as a takeout. **The cue bid in slam bidding is used to pinpoint controls.**

A slam investigation is put into effect after a partnership has determined **the combined hand value and trump holding are adequate** to move toward slam. This will usually be on the 3 or 4 level. The cue bid is used more often when one hand contains a void. Ideally, the partner whose hand contains the void will assume the captaincy.

The cue bid sequence is initiated by bidding the lowest-ranked Ace with each partner continuing to bid up the line. After a 2-club opening bid, the sequence might go as follows:

Opener	Responder
2 clubs	2 diamonds
2 spades	3 spades (sets trump suit)
4 diamonds (denies Ace of clubs)	5 clubs (Ace of clubs)
5 hearts (Ace of hearts)	*5 spades (no more Aces)
6 spades (opener holds spade controls)	

---

*When either partner returns to the trump suit, he has no more Aces. The cue bid is NOT used to show controls in the trump suit. The Grand Slam Force, splinters or Jacoby 2NT may be used to determine the quality of the trump suit.

- If a suit has been skipped during the cue bidding of Aces, one may return to that suit to show the King. For instance, if opener's last bid on the above example had been 6 clubs instead of 6 spades, he would have been showing the King of clubs. If responder now returns to spades, he denies holding a King (or it may put contract level too high).

- A partner may also show a King after his partner has shown the Ace by raising one level. (Partner 5 hearts, you 6 hearts. This denies the ability to cue bid an Ace.)

- After cue bidding toward a slam and all controls have been shown except trumps, a bid of 5NT, called **The Grand Slam Force**, asks partner to bid a grand slam if he holds 2 of the top 3 honor cards in the trump suit. If he doesn't, he signs off at the 6 level and settles for a small slam:

THE GRAND SLAM FORCE

North	**South**
S A K 9 8 7 2	**S** Q J 10 5
H A Q 5 4	**H** K J 10
D K J	**D** --
C Q	**C** A K 5 4 3 2

The Bidding

1 spade	3 spades (traditional)
4 hearts (Ace)	5 clubs (Ace)
5 spades	5 NT (Grand Slam Force)
7 spades	pass

THE BLACKWOOD CONVENTION

Blackwood is played by almost all bridge players. It is used as an effort to reach a makeable slam (or to avoid one that isn't makeable). The Convention was developed by Mr. Easley Blackwood, a well-known player and author. According to Blackwood and to some other authors, the Convention is often misused.

Perhaps it will help to remember that Blackwood is NOT used after notrump openings. Neither is it used after a quantitative notrump bid (1 club – 2 notrump). **Blackwood** is used after a suit has been established as trumps and a partnership has determined that they have adequate strength to move toward a slam. It is **initiated by either partner by a bid of 4NT**. The responses are as follows:

Blackwood	Responder	
4NT	5 clubs	0 or 4 Aces
	5 diamonds	1 Ace
	5 hearts	2 Aces
	5 spades	3 Aces

If the partnership holds all of the Aces, the number of **Kings** can be shown in the **same manner by bidding 5 NT**:

Blackwood	Responder	
5NT	6 clubs	0 or 4 Kings
	6 diamonds	1 King
	6 hearts	2 Kings
	6 spades	3 Kings

Responding to Blackwood with a Void

*To respond with a void, skip one level of bidding.

> With no Aces and a void respond 6 clubs
> With one Ace and a void respond 6 diamonds
> With two Aces and a void respond 6 hearts
> With three Aces and a void respond 6 spades

Partner must be able to figure out from your previous bidding in which suit you are void. If skipping a level puts you above agreed upon trump suit, simply bid 6 of the trump suit.

In his book, Bidding Slams with Blackwood, Mr. Blackwood states one should show a void only if he is sure partner can identify the suit. For instance, one would not show a void in any suit in which his partner has shown strength. IT MUST BE A USEFUL VOID. If you think it isn't useful, simply show the number of Aces held.

Mr. Kantar suggests "If partner **cue bids** your void suit and then bids 4NT, **disregard** the **void** and answer Aces."

For those who wish to really "get down" you may wish to know how to handle interference after a 4NT inquiry. You may answer by using yet other conventions called DOPI (pronounced "dopey") or DEPO, pronounced "depot".

---

* Mr. Kantar and Mr. Root offer a different procedure which is probably more efficient but more difficult to remember in a "heated" bidding session. Their books contain excellent, detailed procedures for bidding, playing and defending.

DOPI

When opponent interferes below the 5 level, use DOPI – after either Blackwood or Gerber.

To show zero or one Ace:

....D double with

....O Aces

....P pass with

....I Ace

To show two Aces, bid next higher suit

To show three Aces, skip a level

You	Opponent	Partner	Opponent
1 heart	pass	4 NT	5 clubs

DOPI

Hand #1	Hand #2	Hand #3	Hand #4
S K 5	S K 5	S A K	S A
H Q 10 9 8 7 6	H A 10 9 8 7 6	H A 10 9 8 7 6	H A Q J 10 9 8
D K Q	D J 10	D Q J	D A 10
C K Q 5	C K Q 5	C K Q 5	C Q 9 4 3
(double)	(pass)	(5 diamonds)	(6 hearts)
0 Aces	1 Ace	2 Aces	3 Aces

DEPO

When opponents interfere above the 5 level, use DEPO which means double with an even number of Aces (or none), pass with an odd number.

You hold:	J 10 8 7	7 6	7 6 5	J 10 9 8	↔ double, none
	A J 6 5	8 7	10 9 8	A J 10 9	↔ double, even
	A J 6 5	7 6	10 9 8	J 10 9 8	↔ pass, odd

TIPS

- Mr. Kantar and Mr. Root suggest **a raise or jump to the 5 level** of agreed-upon trump suits asks you to **bid 6 if you have first- or second-round control of a suit bid by opponent***. If there has been **no interference, the "leap" asks you to bid 6 if you have first- or second-round control of the one unbid suit.** *This shouldn't be confused with a competitive bid at the 5 level (you 1 heart, opponent 4 spades, partner 5 hearts).

- Do not ask for Aces with 2 small cards in an unbid suit unless you have a system for doing so.

- If you find there aren't enough controls for a slam, you may make a bid at the 5 level in a NEW suit to ask partner to sign off in notrump.

  - 4NT
  - 5 clubs
  - 5 any **unbid** suit
  - 5 NT

- Do not use the Grand Slam Force unless you hold 1 of the top 3 honor cards **and** all other side suits are known winners.

- There are various "off shoots" of Blackwood that narrow or refine the responses to Blackwood. Many players agree with Mr. Blackwood and Mr. Root that "plain old Blackwood" serves most players quite well. If one needs to know if partner holds the King and/or Queen in the trump suit, etc., Roman Key Card Blackwood is discussed on the next page.

- Mr. Edwin B. Kantar quips in his wonderful book, <u>A Treasury of Bridge Tips</u>, "if partner can't tell the difference from your previous bidding whether you hold zero or 4 Aces or Kings, either you can't bid or partner can't play".

- Do not count a void as an Ace when responding to Blackwood unless you have a partnership agreement to do so. The value of a void can be included in other ways.

ROMAN KEY CARD BLACKWOOD (RKCB)

Regular Blackwood is simple, but it doesn't address the strength of the combined trump suit. It simply shows the number of Aces and Kings:

4NT	5 clubs	↔	0 or 4 Aces
	5 diamonds	↔	1 Ace
	5 hearts	↔	2 Aces
	5 spades	↔	3 Aces

RKCB allows responder to show the King of the trump suit as a 5th key card. The RKCB also allows responder to show the Queen of the trump suit.

The term "Roman" comes from an Italian team that developed the system. "Key card" refers to the top 3 honors in the trump suit, plus side suit Aces.

R K C B

4NT	5 clubs	↔	0 or 3 key cards
	5 diamonds	↔	1 or 4 key cards
	5 hearts	↔	2 or 5 key cards, without the Queen of trumps
	5 spades	↔	2 or 5 key cards, with the Queen of trumps

If responder bids 5 clubs or 5 diamonds, and the 4NT bidder still wants to know about the Queen of the agreed upon trump suit, he **bids the next suit available.** Responder returns to the trump suit to say no; he bids 6 if he holds the Queen as shown in the following example.

Opener	**Responder**		
1 spade	3 spades	↔	LMR (Limit Major Raise)
4NT (RKCB)	5 clubs	↔	0 or 3 key cards
	5 diamonds	↔	1 or 4 key cards
5 hearts (trump Queen?)	5 spades	↔	No
	6 spades	↔	Yes

THE GERBER CONVENTION

The Gerber Convention, introduced in the U. S. by Mr. John Gerber, is an Ace asking jump bid of 4 clubs used to determine whether a partnership holds adequate top cards (Aces and Kings) to contract for a slam. It is used after an opening NT or a jump rebid at the two level. It can be used by either partner as shown below:

Opener	Responder		Opener Rebid
1 NT	4 clubs		
2 NT	4 clubs		
1 club or diamond	2 NT	↔	*4 clubs

*This is NOT a club rebid; it is Gerber

1 H/S – 2 NT is used for the Jacoby 2NT convention

1 C/D ↔ 3NT ↔ 4 clubs is a slam try in clubs

OR

2 clubs (strong & artificial)	2 diamonds
2 NT (22-24 rebid)	3 clubs, Stayman 3 D/H, transfer 4 clubs, Gerber
3 NT (25-26 rebid)	4 clubs, slam try in clubs 4 D/H, transfer
4 NT (27+ rebid)	Go with 5+ HCP's to NT slam

Responses to the 4-club bid

Gerber	Responder		
4 clubs	4 diamonds	↔	0 or 4 Aces
	4 hearts	↔	1 Ace
	4 spades	↔	2 Aces
	4 NT	↔	3 Aces

- When ALL Aces are held by the partnership, a bid of 5 clubs asks for the number of Kings held:

Gerber	Responder		
5 clubs	5 diamonds	↔	0 or 4 Kings
	5 hearts	↔	1 King
	5 spades	↔	2 Kings
	5 notrump	↔	3 Kings
	6 clubs	↔	4 Kings

TIPS

- Do not ask for Kings unless all Aces are held by the partnership.

- If the Gerber bidder holds all of the Aces, he still goes through the same procedure to inquire about Kings. Therefore, if your partner asks for Kings after finding you have no Aces, you can relax – he has them all.

- The same convention is used to ask for Aces and Kings. In other words, don't use Blackwood and Gerber during the same inquiry.

- DOPI and DEPO may be used with interference after the 4-club bid.

- The same responses apply to a 1NT overcall as apply after a 1NT opening.

- Stayman and Gerber are most compatible in the same bidding process. Stayman is used only after a notrump opening or a jump in notrump. Gerber is used on the 4 level after the first and last notrump bid. **Exception:** After a game bid of 3 NT, 4 clubs is a slam try in clubs.

Declarer South 6 Hearts
North-South Vulnerable

Slam Bidding
Blackwood

North (dealer)
S 10 5
H A 6
D K Q J
C K Q J 10 9 4

West
S K 7 4
H 5 4
D 10 9 8 7 3
C A 6 2

East
S Q 8 6 3 2
H 9 8 2
D 5 4
C 7 5 3

South
S A J 9
H K Q J 10 7 3
D A 6 2
C 8

The Bidding: North 1 club – East pass – South 1 heart – West pass – North 3 clubs – East pass – South 3 hearts – West pass – North 4 hearts – East pass – South 4NT – West pass – North 5 diamonds – East pass – South 6 hearts – West pass, pass, pass.

The Lead: The 4 of spades

The Play: South wins the spade lead – draws outstanding trumps and leads a small club toward the dummy. West must play second hand high, cash the King of spades and take pride in his **plan** to defeat the contract.

Tips: Bridge is not an exact science. We must make a plan for defense as well as for the play. Listen to the bidding – do some counting – BEFORE the attack!

One doesn't usually lead from an unprotected honor when defending a slam bid. Since N/S showed 2 strong suits, West was trying to set up a trick early before declarer forced out his Ace of clubs. Use aggressive defense when opponents have shown two strong suits.

Declarer South 6 NT
Both Non-Vulnerable

Slam Bidding
Gerber

North (dealer)
S K 8 2
H A Q
D A Q 6
C A 8 7 4 3

West
S A 10
H 10 9 8 5
D 10 7 4 3 2
C Q J

East
S 9 7 6 4 3
H 7 4 3 2
D J 5
C 6 2

South
S Q J 5
H K J 6
D K 9 8
C K 10 9 5

The Bidding: North 1 club – East pass – South 2 NT – West pass – North 4 clubs – East pass – South 4 diamonds – West pass – North 6NT – East pass, pass, pass.

The Lead: The 10 of hearts

The Play: Win with the Ace of hearts in dummy. Play the Queen of hearts to unblock. Play a small club to the King, and the 10 of clubs to the Ace, a small club to the 9 – preserving the 5 to reach the 8. Next play a small spade to the King. If the Ace isn't taken, abandon spades and discard one on the King of hearts and one on the long club.

Tips: Gerber is used after a notrump opening bid or a quantitative notrump bid (1 club – 2 NT) as shown in this hand.

Even though North opened with a club bid and later jumped in clubs, he is NOT showing interest in the club suit as trumps. His 4-club bid is GERBER.

Declarer South 7 Hearts
North-South Vulnerable

Slam Bidding
Blackwood

North
S 7 6 3
H 5 2
D A K Q J 5 2
C 9 8

West
S 10 9 8 5 2
H 8 3
D 8 7 3
C Q J 10

East
S Q 4
H 9 4
D 9 6 4
C K 7 6 5 3 2

South (dealer)
S A K J
H A K Q J 10 7 6
D 10
C A 4

The Bidding: South 2 clubs – West pass – North 3 diamonds – East pass – South 4 hearts – West pass – North 4NT – East pass – South 5 spades – West pass – North 7 hearts – East pass, pass, pass.

The Lead: The Queen of clubs

The Play: South wins the club lead, draws trumps and discards losers on North's diamond suit.

Tips: The rare jump bid by the opening 2-club bidder promises a self-sufficient trump suit. It is NOT strength showing other than in trumps. The opener is simply saying "don't let the value of your trump suit slow you down, I've got 'it' covered even if you are void."

A responder can give a positive bid with 8 or more points and a 5-card suit containing 2 honors. Since 2 diamonds is a negative and/or a waiting bid, North jumped the level of bidding to show a positive bid in the diamond suit.

Declarer South 6 NT
North-South Vulnerable

Slam Bidding
Direct

North
S 8 5 3
H 9 5
D 4
C A K J 7 5 3 2

West
S 10 6 4 2
H 10 8 7 4 3
D J 6
C Q 8

East (dealer)
S 9 7
H K J
D K 10 9 8 5 3 2
C 10 9

South
S A K Q J
H A Q 6 2
D A Q 7
C 6 4

The Bidding: East 3 diamonds – South 4 diamonds – West pass – North 6 clubs – East pass – South 6 NT – West pass, pass, pass.

The Lead: The Jack of diamonds

The Play: Declarer needs to bring in the club suit to make his contract. There are 4 cards missing in the suit; therefore South should make a safety play in clubs. He wins with the Queen of diamonds, plays a small club from BOTH hands in the event they are 3/1.

Tips: Many times a declarer must develop an entry to dummy ... either in a side suit, in the trump suit, or by a safety play as shown here.

How did South know North had the AK of clubs? He didn't know for sure. That's what preempts do to you. When North jumped the level of bidding, South gambled on a NT slam ... especially since a diamond lead was expected. Don't be a "scaredy cat" ... bid them up ... play them well!

South's cue bid is the strongest call one can make after opponents opens with a preempt. It usually shows values for a 2-club opening.

Declarer South 7 Spades
North-South Vulnerable

Slam Bidding
Blackwood

North
S K Q J 10 3
H A K 9 8 4 3
D K
C 3

West
S 9 7 2
H 10 2
D Q 5 4 3
C Q J 10 9

East (dealer)
S 8
H J 7 6 5
D J 10 9 2
C 8 7 6 2

South
S A 6 5 4
H Q
D A 8 7 6
C A K 5 4

The Bidding: East pass – South 1 diamond – West pass – North 1 heart – East pass – South 1 spade – West pass – North 4NT – East pass – South 5 spades – West pass – North 7 spades – East pass, pass, pass.

The Lead: The Queen of clubs

The Play: Win the club lead, play the Queen of hearts. Lead a small spade to the board, play a <u>small</u> heart and trump it with the Ace. Unblock the King of diamonds. Draw the outstanding trumps and discard losers on the established hearts and the trump suit.

Tips: Declarer makes his hand dummy and uses partner's as the master hand. A "dummy reversal" occurs when there are plenty of trumps between the two hands; but, dummy's are stronger AND contain a long, outside suit on which declarer can discard losers.

There is no need to consider ruffing small diamonds and clubs since there are long suits on which to discard.

Declarer South 6 Spades
East-West Vulnerable

Slam Bidding
Direct

North (dealer)
S K 6 5
H A Q 10 3
D A K 9 8 4
C 2

West
S 9 8 4 2
H 4
D J 7 5
C K 8 5 4 3

East
S 7 3
H 9 8 7 6 5
D Q 6
C Q J 9 6

South
S A Q J 10
H K J 2
D 10 3 2
C A 10 7

The Bidding: North 1 diamond – East pass – South 1 spade – West pass – North 2 hearts* – East pass – South 4 hearts – West pass – North 6 spades – East pass, pass, pass.

The Lead: The 4 of clubs

The Play: South wins in his hand and trumps a club in dummy … comes back to his hand with a trump and ruffs another club. He now allows opponents to win a diamond trick, playing low from both hands. South wins any return and draws outstanding trumps.

Tips: North had compensating values, so he felt it was safe to support spades with only 3 cards in the suit.

On every hand, be aware of how each suit will break – most especially – the trump suit. It is also important to execute each play at the right time to avoid losing control of the trump suit. Note declarer needs all 4 trumps to draw all of West's trumps, thus the safety play in diamonds.

*A reverse bid forcing one round

Declarer South 6 NT
North-South Vulnerable

Slam Bidding
The Gerber Convention

North
S K Q J
H A J 5
D K Q 3
C Q 10 7 5

West
S 10 9 8 6
H 8 6
D 7 4
C J 8 4 3 2

East
S A 5 4
H 10 9 7 3 2
D 10 8 6 2
C 9

South (dealer)
S 7 3 2
H K Q 4
D A J 9 5
C A K 6

The Bidding: South 1NT – West pass – North 4 clubs – East pass – South 4 spades – West pass – North 6NT – East pass, pass, pass.

The Lead: The 10 of spades

The Play: South can count eleven winners. South plays the Ace and King of clubs; when East shows out, he can safely finesse West for the Jack.

Tips: The Gerber bidders don't ask for Kings unless the partnership holds all of the Aces.

When trying to get the count on the whole hand or 1 suit, concentrate primarily on one opponent's hand.

A notrump opener plus a notrump opener usually equals a slam.

68

Declarer South 6 NT
Both Vulnerable

Slam Bidding
Direct

North
S K 9
H A J 4
D K Q 10
C Q 10 9 8 7

West
S 7 6 3 2
H 8 7 6 5
D 8 7 3 2
C A

East
S 10 5 4
H 3 2
D 6 5 4
C 6 5 4 3 2

South (dealer)
S A Q J 8
H K Q 10 9
D A J 9
C K J

The Bidding: South 2NT – West pass – North 6 NT – pass, pass, pass.

The Lead: Top of nothing

The Play: Win the lead and play clubs remembering to play high cards from short side first.

Tips: Holding a 15 HCP hand plus a 5-card suit, there is little doubt a slam bid is going to be successful. North simply adds his HCP's to those shown by South's bid (20 + 15) = 35 HCP's. There can be no more than 1 Ace missing from the combined hands. North may have thought his hand was too balanced to try for 7NT. With so many fillers and the 5-card suit – many North's will try for a "Grand".

There is one great advantage to the direct slam bid. The opponents can't gain much insight on the best lead.

Declarer South 6 Spades
North-South Vulnerable

Slam Bidding
Direct

North
S K 10
H 10 5 2
D Q J 9
C A 10 8 3 2

West
S 6 5
H 7
D K 10 6 4 2
C Q 9 7 6 4

East
S 2
H Q J 9 8 6
D 8 7 5 3
C K J 5

South (dealer)
S A Q J 9 8 7 4 3
H A K 4 3
D A
C --

The Bidding: South 2 clubs – West pass – North 3 clubs – East pass – South 3 spades – West pass – North 3NT – East pass – South 6 spades – West pass, pass, pass.

The Lead: The 7 of hearts

The Play: Win the heart lead, play the Ace of diamonds, go to the board, draw trumps, play the Ace of clubs and discard a small **heart**. Play the Queen of diamonds and discard another heart … a loser on a loser play.

Tip: Had East played the King of diamonds, declarer could ruff. This is called a **ruffing finesse**.

Declarer South 6 Spades
Both Vulnerable

Slam Bidding
Not So Grand

North
S K 10 4 2
H 9 5
D Q 7
C A Q 5 3 2

West
S A
H 7 6 2
D 9 8 6 5 4
C K J 9 4

East
S 7 3
H 10 4 3
D J 10 3 2
C 10 8 7 6

South (dealer)
S Q J 9 8 6 5
H A K Q J 8
D A K
C --

The Bidding: South 2 clubs – West pass – North 3 clubs – East pass – South 3 spades – West pass – North 4 spades – East pass – South *5 NT – West pass – North 6 spades – East pass, pass, pass.

The Lead: The 9 of diamonds

The Play: Win and draw trumps – the rest is easy.

Tips: The *5NT bid by South is the Grand Slam Force which asks partner to bid 7 of the agreed-upon trump suit if he holds 2 of the top 3 honor cards or to sign off in 6 if he doesn't. North dutifully signs off in 6 spades since he holds only 1.

Once responder gives a positive bid showing a minimum of 8 HCP's, the 2-club bidder is committed to game and usually starts thinking SLAM!

Declarer South 7 Spades
East-West Vulnerable

Slam Bidding
Cue Bids* and **Grand Slam Force

North
S K Q 5 4 3
H A K Q 7
D K 6 5 4
C --

West
S 2
H J 10 9 5
D 10 8 7
C Q 8 7 6 2

East
S 7 6
H 4 3 2
D J 9 3
C J 9 5 4 3

South (dealer)
S A J 10 9 8
H 8 6
D A Q 2
C A K 10

The Bidding: South 1 spade – West pass – North 3 spades – East pass – South 4 clubs – West pass – North *4 hearts – East pass – South **5 NT – West pass – North 7 spades – East pass, pass, pass.

The Lead: The Jack of hearts

Tips: The one who knows, goes!

Either North or South may initiate a cue bidding sequence and/or the Grand Slam Force.

The Grand Slam Force is instigated by a call of 5NT. It asks partner to bid 7 of the agreed upon trump suit if he holds 2 of the top 3 honors and to sign off in 6 if he doesn't.

North's 3-spade bid is traditional. If using Jacoby 2NT, his call would be 2NT showing game-going values and very good trump support.

Declarer South 7 Spades
North-South Vulnerable

Slam Bidding
Blackwood
DOPI, double with <u>0</u>, pass with <u>1</u> – bid the next available suit with <u>2</u>, skip a level with <u>3</u>*

North
S K Q 10 8 5 2
H K Q J 3
D A
C K 3

West
S 6 3
H 9 8 5 4
D 7
C 10 9 7 5 4 2

East
S --
H 7 6
D K Q J 10 9 4 3 2
C Q 8 6

South (dealer)
S A J 9 7 4
H A 10 2
D 8 6 5
C A J

The Bidding: South 1 spade – West pass – North 4NT – East 5 diamonds –
*South 6 spades – West pass – North 7 spades – East pass, pass, pass.

The Lead: The 7 of diamonds

The Play: Easy!

Tip: The need for DOPI is rare; but, it's a great gadget when opponents interfere with slam inquiries – and they do!

Declarer East 5 Spades Doubled
Both Vulnerable

Slam Bidding
Double with 0, Pass with 1*
Blackwood

North
S 6
H K J 10 8 7 2
D 6 4
C A K 8 7

West
S Q 8 5 4
H 3
D 10 9 8 7 3
C 10 4 3

East
S K J 10 9 7 3 2
H 6
D A 2
C J 5 2

South (dealer)
S A
H A Q 9 5 4
D K Q J 5
C Q 9 6

The Bidding: South 1 heart – West pass – North 3 hearts – East 3 spades – South 4 NT – West 5 spades – North pass* – East pass – South double** – West pass, pass, pass.

The Lead: The Ace of hearts

The Play: North discards the 2 of hearts, suggesting South lead a club. When South wins the third club, he switches to the King of diamonds.

Tips: Playing *DOPI, North's pass over West's 5 spades shows 1 Ace.

West's 5-spade bid made it impossible to know whether a slam was available. South tries a penalty double since he didn't know whether North's Ace was in clubs or diamonds. Since South held losers in the club suit, he might have cue bid spades instead of bidding 4 NT. North would now cue bid clubs and the "good" slam would have been reached.

**penalty double

Declarer South 6 Hearts
East-West Vulnerable

Slam Bidding
The Cue Bid

North (dealer)
S A 8 5
H 7 4 2
D K 6 3
C 7 5 3 2

West
S 9 7 6 4
H Q
D 9 8 7 5 4
C Q J 10

East
S 10 3 2
H 10 9 8 5
D 10
C K 9 8 6 4

South
S K Q J
H A K J 6 3
D A Q J 2
C A

The Bidding: North pass – East pass – South 2 clubs – West pass – North
2 diamonds – East pass – South 2 hearts – West pass – North *3 hearts – East
pass – South 4 clubs – West pass – North 4 spades – East pass – South
5 diamonds – West pass – North **6 diamonds – East pass – South 6 hearts –
West pass, pass, pass.

The Lead: The Queen of clubs

The Play: When West played the Queen of trumps under declarer's Ace, it was
obvious declarer must lose a trump. He therefore concentrated on avoiding a
diamond loser. While declarer is playing diamonds, East may take his winner or
not. That is his only trick.

Tips: Any time there is one high trump out against a contract, just play normally
until opponent ruffs in.

The Ace of trumps is not shown with a cue bid. When either of the
partnership returns to the agreed upon trump suit, he is saying he has no other
outside Ace.

 *Three hearts here is stronger than 4 hearts.

**When either partner bypasses a suit while cue bidding and later bids that suit,
he is showing the King. When a raise of a cue bid is made, it shows the King
and denies the holding of another Ace.

Declarer South 6 Spades, doubled
Both Vulnerable

Slam Bidding
Blackwood
DEPO, double* with even (0-2-4) pass with odd (1 or 3)
Lightner Slam Double**

North
S A K 7 6
H K Q J 9 4 3 2
D 4
C 2

West
S 4
H 10 8 7 5
D 2
C A Q J 10 9 8 7

East
S 5 3 2
H --
D K J 10 8 7 3 2
C K 6 5 4

South (dealer)
S Q J 10 9 8
H A 6
D A Q 9 6 5
C 3

The Bidding: South 1 spade – West 3 clubs – North 4 NT – East 6 clubs – South double* – West pass – North 6 spades – East double ** – pass, pass, pass.

The Lead: The 10 of hearts

The Play: East trumps the heart, plays a small club to West; West leads another heart for East to ruff – down 2. Good defense!

Tips: An interference at or above 5NT is handled by DEPO which takes up less bidding room than DOPI.

   **When a slam bid is doubled, the doubler is asking for an unusual lead – never trumps, never the suit bid by doubler's partnership. Sometimes – but not always – the first bid suit of dummy in a suit bid. West chose hearts because they were longer. The double is known as "Lightner Slam Double".

CHAPTER FOUR: MAJOR SUITS

Bridge is a game of the majors! Since a contract in the majors has evolved as the ultimate contract, there have been numerous gadgets developed to precisely define major suit values. One of the most popular is the **Limit Major Raise** (LMR). It is used only with the 5-card major system.

Traditionally, a jump raise after partner opens 1 heart or 1 spade is unlimited in HCP's and game forcing. This often leads to confusion for responder when he holds good trump support but only 10-11 points. It's too many points for a simple raise (6-9) and not enough for a forcing raise (13+). Using standard methods, responder must "borrow" a new suit to show pointcount and then support partner. The LMR makes life easier. It precisely describes hand value and preempts fourth chair.

THE LIMIT MAJOR RAISE (LMR)

The LMR used after partner opens 1 heart or 1 spade is a **3-level non-forcing raise.** It **shows 4 cards** in the trump suit (or 3 very good ones) and **exactly 10-11 points** including dummy's distributional values. Experienced players tend to open some hands with less than 13 points. If partner opens a major using the Rule of 15, the Rule of 20, or any other gadget with less than 13 points, he may pass your LMR.

Summary
The Limit Major Raise

- The LMR is used only with the 5-card major system.

- The LMR shows 4-card trump support and exactly 10-11 points including dummy's distributional values. It is highly invitational but not forcing.

- *If opponent interferes, the LMR may still be used as shown above. A partnership may choose to adopt the *Jordan 2NT Convention to make it more difficult for fourth seat to enter the bidding and/or to further describe hand value.

- Responder uses splinter bids, Jacoby 2NT or the "traditional" route with strong hands.

EXAMPLES
Limit Major Raises

Example #1		Example #2	
Opener	Responder	Opener	Responder
S A J 10 5 4	S K Q 3 2	S A K 10 9 8	S Q 6 5 4
H K Q	H A 5 4	H K Q 2	H 10 6 3
D Q 5 4 3	D J 10 8	D A 10 8 6	D K Q
C 10 9	C 7 6 3	C 8	C K 5 4 2
1 spade	3 spades	1 spade	3 spades
pass		4 spades	

Jordan 2NT Convention

* If right-hand opponent makes an interfering bid after partner opens

1 heart or 1 spade, third seat may use the Jordan 2 NT Convention to show a

LMR and 3 of the suit as preemptive.

Declarer South 3 Hearts
None Vulnerable

The Limit Major Raise

<u>North</u>
S Q 4
H K Q 5 4
D 9 8 4 3
C K 5 4

<u>West</u>
S K 10 9 8 2
H A 3
D J 10 2
C 8 7 6

<u>East</u>
S 7 6 5 3
H 6 2
D A 7 6
C A J 10 9

<u>South</u> (dealer)
S A J
H J 10 9 8 7
D K Q 5
C Q 3 2

<u>**The Bidding:**</u> South 1 heart – West pass – North 3 hearts – East pass, pass, pass.

<u>**The Lead:**</u> The Jack of diamonds

<u>**The Play:**</u> East wins the diamond and returns a low spade. When South draws trumps he might try setting up a long diamond for a discard.

<u>**Tip:**</u> The LMR alerts South right away that a game level contract is out of his reach.

Declarer South 6 Hearts
None Vulnerable

The Limit Major Raise

North
S A 9
H Q 9 5 4
D Q J 10 9
C J 3 2

West
S K Q J 8 7 6
H --
D 5 4 3 2
C Q 10 4

East
S 5 4 3 2
H 10 3 2
D K 7 6
C 8 7 6

South (dealer)
S 10
H A K J 8 7 6
D A 8
C A K 9 5

The Bidding: South 1 heart – West 1 spade – North 3 hearts – East pass – South 4 clubs – West pass – North 4 spades – East pass – South 6 hearts – West pass, pass, pass.

The Lead: The King of spades

The Play: Declarer wins the spade lead and plays the Queen of diamonds. If East doesn't cover, declarer finesses again but must play the Ace. Declarer draws trumps and plays another diamond. He ruffs and discards a losing club on the fourth diamond. This is called "a ruffing finesse".

Tip: Declarer knows only 2 of partner's 10 HCP's are in the heart suit; therefore, either the club or diamond suit will develop for discards.

Declarer North 4 Spades
None Vulnerable

The Limit Major Raise

North (dealer)
S A K 10 9 8 7
H 10
D A J
C Q J 9 8

West
S 3 2
H A J 8 7 6
D 10 4 3 2
C A 6

East
S 5
H 9 5 4
D K Q 6 5
C 10 5 4 3 2

South
S Q J 6 4
H K Q 3 2
D 9 8 7
C K 7

The Bidding: North 1 spade – East pass – South 3 spades – West pass – North 4 spades – East pass, pass, pass.

The Lead: The King of diamonds

The Play: Win the diamond, draw trumps, and develop the club suit.

Tip: How would you respond to the spade opener without the LMR?

JACOBY 2 NT

Jacoby 2 NT is an exploratory bid. It asks partner to further describe his hand after his opening bid of 1 heart or 1 spade. Jacoby 2NT is a **game-force bid** with slam possibilities "in the air". This convention often allows a partnership to bid a slam with less than the requisite 33 points. Jacoby 2NT is not related to the Jacoby transfer; but, it too was introduced in the U.S. by Mr. Jacoby. The pointcount required picks up where the Limit Major Raise ends.

It is used after partner has opened on the one level in either major.

Example: Partner 1 heart – You 2 NT:

Jacoby 2 NT shows:

- Game-forcing values (13+) (or a very good 12)
- Trump support (4 cards) (or 3 very good ones)

Jacoby 2 NT asks:

- The shape of partner's hand regardless of strength i.e., shortness or length in a side suit.

The 2NT bid may not be used unless the above criteria are met. With game-going values without trump support, use the traditional methods to find a landing spot.

Summary
The Jacoby 2NT Response to a Major-Suit Opening

- Its purpose is to explore for a slam.

- It shows 13+ points including values for shortness (no upward limit).

- It **is not used** by a passed hand.

- It **is used** with an intervening double, since the bidding level will not have changed.

- If opponents intervene with an overcall, the bidding reverts to standard:
    - A double is for penalty
    - A new suit bid is exploratory and forcing
    - A notrump bid shows a stopper in opponent's suit

The Opener's Rebid

- Cue bid any side suit singleton or a void

- With 12-14, rebid 4 H/S

- With 15-17, rebid 3 NT

- With 18+, **rebid the agreed upon suit** (1 heart – 2 NT – 3 hearts)

- With a **good** 5-card side suit (A Q 10 9 8), jump bid to the 4 level (1 S–2 NT–4 C/D/H) even with a singleton or void.

- With a **weak** 5-card side suit PLUS a singleton or void, prefer showing shortness on the three level.

The 2 NT Bidder's Rebid

The responder becomes captain after opener has described his hand. He

may proceed as follows:

- Sign off at the 4 level
- Begin a cue bid sequence showing Aces (opener then cue bids any Ace)
- Bid a slam

Interference should not necessarily impede responses.

Declarer South 6 Hearts

None Vulnerable

Jacoby 2NT
Opener has Singleton
and Strong Hand

North
S A 10
H A 5 3 2
D K J 10
C K 5 4 3

West
S Q J 8 4
H 7 6
D 3 2
C A 9 8 7 6

East
S 9 7 6 5
H 9 8
D 7 6 5 4
C Q J 10

South (dealer)
S K 3 2
H K Q J 10 4
D A Q 9 8
C 2

The Bidding: South 1 heart – West pass – North 2 NT – East pass – South 3 clubs* -- West pass – North 3 spades** – East pass – South 4 diamonds*** – West pass – North 6 hearts– East pass, pass, pass.

*A singleton or void **cue bid ***cue bid

The Lead: The Ace of clubs (South showed a singleton or void.)

The Play: Declarer wins the second club, discarding a small spade, draws trumps and claims.

Tip: Declarer must show his hand and tell how he would handle any losers. Make sure all the trumps are in before claiming. Opponents may ask you to play the hand out. You must!

Declarer South 6 Spades
None Vulnerable

Jacoby 2NT
Opener has Balanced Hand

North
S K J 10 5 4
H A 5
D A 6
C Q J 10 2

West
S 2
H J 10 9 6
D K Q J 7
C 9 8 7 6

East
S 6 3
H K 7 8 2
D 10 9 8 4
C 5 4 3

South (dealer)
S A Q 9 8 7
H Q 4 3
D 5 3 2
C A K

The Bidding: South 1 spade – West pass – North 2 NT* – East pass – South 3 NT** – West pass – North 4 NT*** – East pass – South 5 hearts – West pass – North 6 spades – East pass, pass, pass.

*Jacoby 2NT – **Balanced hand 15-17 HCP's – *** Blackwood

The Lead: The King of diamonds

The Play: Win the diamond lead, draw trumps and establish the club suit for discards by unblocking the AK of clubs. Discard 2 hearts and concede 1 diamond.

Tip: The responder shows an opening hand and 13+ points when he bids 2 NT after a 1 H/S opening. The 3 NT rebid by opener shows pointcount; it is not to play since a trump fit is known.

Declarer South 4 Spades
None Vulnerable

Jacoby 2NT
Opener has Minimum Hand

North
S A K 3
H Q 10
D A 9 6 4
C Q J 10 9

West
S 5 2
H A K 7 5 4
D 5 3 2
C 8 6 2

East
S 9 7 4
H J 6 3 2
D Q J
C 7 5 4 3

South (dealer)
S Q J 10 8 6
H 9 8
D K 10 8 7
C A K

The Bidding: South 1 spade – West pass – North 2 NT – East pass – South 4 spades – West pass, pass, pass.

The Lead: The Ace of hearts

The Play: When declarer gains the lead, he draws trumps, unblocks the AK of clubs, goes to the board and discards 2 diamonds on the good clubs.

Tip: South's rebid to game is the weakest response to Jacoby 2 NT. He has a minimum hand with no singleton or void.

Declarer South 6 Spades
None Vulnerable

Jacoby 2NT
Opener has Good 5-Card Side Suit

North
S A K 9
H A 10
D 9 6 4
C Q J 10 9 8

West
S 5 2
H K Q 8 7 5 4
D Q 3 2
C 6 2

East
S 7 4 3
H J 6 3 2
D J 5
C 7 5 4 3

South (dealer)
S Q J 10 8 6
H 9
D A K 10 8 7
C A K

The Bidding: South 1 spade – West pass – North 2 NT – East pass – South 4 diamonds – West pass – North 4 NT – East pass – South 5 hearts – West pass – North 6 spades – East pass, pass, pass.

The Lead: The King of hearts

The Play: Declarer wins the heart lead, draws trumps, unblocks the AK of clubs and discards losers on the club suit.

Tip: When holding a maximum hand, priority is given to showing a good 5-card side suit over showing shortness.

SPLINTER BIDS

Dorothy Hayden Truscott, a famous bridge author and player, introduced splinter bids in 1964. The splinter bid – a game force call – shows 4-card trump support, 13-16 points and a singleton or void in the suit splintered. It is shown by a <u>double</u> jump to the suit containing a singleton or a void. The bid is a convenient adjunct to other major suit raises as shown below:

Responses to a 5-Card Major Suit Opening

- A simple raise
  3-card support, 6-9(10) points.

- A jump raise (LMR)
  4-card support, exactly
  10-11 points.

- A jump bid to 2 NT (Jacoby)
  4-card support, a minimum of
  12 points, no upward limit.

- A double jump bid (splinter)
  (1 heart, 4 clubs) 13-16 points,
  4-card trump support, a singleton or
  void in the suit splintered.

Examples

Partner	You
S A 10 9 8 7	**S** K Q 3 2
H A 5	**H** --
D Q J 10 8	**D** A K 7 6 5
C A K	**C** 10 9 8 7

The Bid:
1 spade	**4 hearts (splinter)**
5 clubs (cue bid, Ace)	5 diamonds (cue bid, Ace)
5 hearts (cue bid Ace)	5 spades (no more Aces)
6 spades	

- A slam with 30 HCP's

	Partner	You
	S A 5	**S** K Q J
	H K J 10 9 8	**H** A Q 5 4
	D K Q 5 2	**D** J 10 9 4
	C 10 9	**C** 7
The Bid:	**1 heart**	**4 clubs**
	4 spades – Ace	5 hearts – no outside Ace
	pass	pass

The hand has two losers, a club and a diamond.

The opener may also splinter if responder goes to the two level in a new suit. If responder doesn't splinter, use the Limit Major Raise or Jacoby 2 NT, the opener knows he has 10+ points but inadequate support for the major suit opened. **If the opener has excellent support for partner's suit, a singleton or void in any other suit and a minimum of 4 cards – then he may splinter:**

Example

	Opener	Responder
	S A K J 10 9	**S** 7 6
	H K Q J 4	**H** A 10 9 8 7
	D K 9 7	**D** A Q 2
	C 10	**C** Q 5 4 3
The Bid:	**1 spade**	**2 hearts**
	*4 clubs	4 diamonds (Ace)
	6 hearts	

- A slam with 29 HCP's

	Opener	Responder
	S A 5 2	**S** K J 10
	H K Q J 10 9	**H** A 2
	D Q J 10 8 7	**D** A K 9 6 5
	C --	**C** Q J 8
The Bid:	**1 heart**	**2 diamonds**
	**4 clubs	4 hearts (Ace)
	*5 NT	7 diamonds

- A grand slam with 30 HCP's!
* Grand Slam Force
** Discuss with partners to avoid one interpreting this as a jump shift.

The opener may also splinter a one-level response by partner; but, he **must** have 18+ HCP's since partner could have a minimum hand as shown following:

Opener	**Responder**
S K J 10 9	**S** A Q 8 7 6
H A Q J 10 9	**H** 5
D A K J 6	**D** Q J 10 9
C --	**C** 10 8 2

The Bid:
	1 heart	**1 spade**
	4 clubs (singleton or void)	4 spades (back to the agreed upon suit, no outside Aces)
		5 diamonds
	4 NT	
	6 spades	

- A slam with 28 HCP's

Opener	**Responder**
S A 5	**S** K J 10
H A K J 10 9	**H** Q
D Q J 10 8 7 4	**D** A K 9 6 5
C --	**C** Q J 8 2

The Bid:
	1 diamond	**3 hearts**
	4 clubs (singleton or void)	4 diamonds (no more Aces)
	5 NT (GSF)**	7 diamonds

- A grand slam with 31 HCP's!
- ** Grand Slam Force

Tips
Splinter Bids

- The splinter by responder shows 13-16 points, including distribution.
- A splinter bid by opener shows 18+ points (enough for game if responder's hand is minimum.)
- Do not splinter with a singleton Ace or King so that partner can judge your HCP's.
- Do not splinter past game.
- As always, if responder holds a monster hand, the bidding progresses slowly. Use Jacoby 2 NT with more than 16 points since the pointcount is unlimited on the 2 NT call.
- When responder goes directly to game after partner has splintered, he has nothing more to offer.
- The **splinter** is still **on** after a **double**. The **splinter** is **off** after an opposing overcall and the bidding reverts to standard.

CHAPTER FIVE: MINOR SUITS

THE INVERTED MINOR

The inverted minor is a "survivor" i.e. a feature of the Kaplan-Sheinwold

system of bidding developed years ago.

When responder gives a simple raise 1 club – 2 clubs, the opponents will

invariably intervene. If the meaning of the raise is inverted (reversed) and **the**

2-club response is strong, it does have a preemptive effect because

responder's hand value is unknown. The **primary** purpose, however, is to find a

3NT contract on a low level when a partnership owns 8+ cards in either minor

suit.

- A jump bid (1 C/D-3 C/D) shows 6-9 HCP's, 5 cards in the trump suit (or 4 good ones), and is not forcing. If opener has a very strong hand, he may make another call, which of course would be forcing. 1 club-3 clubs-3 spades (opener) – your bid should be 3NT or 4 clubs.

- A simple minor suit raise, 1 C/D-2 C/D, shows 10+ HCP's (no upper limit) and a 5+card suit. Forcing one round.

- The responder denies a 4-card major AND the ability to give an immediate 2NT response after partner opens 1 club or 1 diamond.

- An intervening bid doesn't necessarily change the bidding. Discuss with partner.

- A cue bid of opponent's suit is the Western Cue Bid Convention (see page 94).

Examples
Hand #1

	Opener	Responder
	S K 9 5	S A J 8
	H Q J 10	H 10 8
	D A 9 4	D K J 5
	C A K Q 9	C Q J 10 8 5
The Bid:	**1 club**	**2 clubs**
Rebids:	3 NT	pass

Opener has all suits stopped and a nice club holding.

Hand #2

	S K Q	S A 5
	H 9 8 7 6	H Q J 3
	D K J 8	D 10 5 4
	C Q J 6 5	C A K 10 9 8
The Bid:	**1 club**	**2 clubs**
Rebids;	2 diamonds	3 NT

Opener bid the one suit responder needed to know about.

Hand #3

	Opener	Responder
	S J 10 9 8	S A K 7
	H A 9 8 7	H Q 6 5
	D A K J 4	D Q 9 8 7 6
	C 10	C 8 7
The Bid:	**1 diamond**	**2 diamonds**
Rebids:	2 hearts	2 spades
	3 diamonds	Pass

- Neither partner has a club stopper on the above hand so the contract should be in diamonds.
- When either partner returns to the minor suit or 2 NT he has told his story.
- If opponents interfere, the inverted minor can still be used. Just ignore the bid if you still have NT on the "agenda" after hearing opponent's suit.

92

Declarer North 3 NT
None Vulnerable

The Inverted Minor

North (dealer)
S K J 2
H A 10 9
D K 5 4
C J 10 9 8

West
S A Q 8 7
H 5 4 3 2
D Q J 10 8
C 2

East
S 6 5 4 3
H Q 8 7 6
D 7 6
C Q 7 6

South
S 10 9
H K J
D A 9 3 2
C A K 5 4 3

The Bidding: North 1 club – East pass – South 2 clubs – West pass – North 2 NT (shows minimum hand) – East pass – South 3 diamonds – West pass – North 3 NT – East pass, pass, pass.

The Lead: The 6 of hearts

The Play: Play the Jack, overtake with the Ace, play the Jack of clubs and let it ride. Repeat the finesse until the Queen appears.

Tip: South's 3 diamond bid showed extra values.

Declarer North 3 NT
None Vulnerable

The Inverted Minor

North
S K Q 4
H A 10 8
D K 8 7
C A Q 6 2

West (dealer)
S 5 2
H Q 9 7 5 4 3 2
D 6 3 2
C 5

East
S A J 7 6 3
H --
D Q J 10 9 5
C 7 4 3

South
S 10 9 8
H K J 6
D A 4
C K J 10 9 8

The Bidding: West pass – North 1 club – East 1 spade – South 2 spades* –
West pass – North 3 NT – East pass, pass, pass.

The Lead: The Queen of diamonds

The Play: Declarer wins in dummy and finesses for the Queen of hearts. He
might now play toward the KQ of spades. If East doesn't take his Ace, declarer
abandons spades and runs the winners.

Tip: Partnerships playing inverted minors may bid 2- or 3-card suits to explore
for game after the two-level raise.

* Western Cue Bid, next page

THE WESTERN CUE BID

The Western Cue Bid is used after partner opens on the one level and the next opponent overcalls. Responder bids the same suit the opponent overcalled. to **ask** partner if he has a stopper for notrump.

The cue bidder will often have minor suit support for partner's opening bid and enough HCP's to go to game if partner has the much needed stopper. Responder must have the two unbid suits stopped and less than 3-card support for partner's major suit opening.

Examples

Opener	**Opponent**	**Responder**
S A J 10 9 8		S K 4
H Q 10 9 8		H J 6 5
D A K 5		D Q J 9 8
C 10 8		C A K 4

The Bid:	**1 spade**	**2 hearts**	**3 hearts**
	3 NT		pass

Opener	**Opponent**	**Responder**
S Q 9		S K J 4
H A 6 4		H 10 9 8
D Q J 9		D A 5
C A 10 9 7 6		C K Q 5 4 2

The Bid:	**1 club**	**1 heart**	**2 hearts**
	2 NT	pass	3 NT

Responder usually needs 3 cards to the 10 or Jack in opponent's suit to use the Western Cue.

CHAPTER SIX: PREEMPTIVE BIDDING

THREE-LEVEL PREEMPTS

The purpose of a preemptive bid is to obstruct opponents' normal bidding sequence, to suggest a sacrifice contract and/or to announce to partner that the hand is offensive as opposed to defensive.

A 3-level preemptive bid shows 11 HCP's or a little less, and a suit of at least **7 cards.** A 4-level preempt shows 8 cards. A game-bid in the minors shows 8 or 9 cards. Most of the HCP's are in the suit preempted.

Non-vulnerable bidders can be much more aggressive, especially when opponents are vulnerable.

Non-Vulnerable	**Vulnerable**
S K J 9 8 7 6 5	**S** A K 8 7 6 5 4
H 5 4	**H** Q
D A 5 2	**D** J 10 9
C 10	**C** 7 6
Open 3 spades	**Open 3 spades**

The Rule of Two and Three is a good guideline for opening. The preempter can afford to be defeated **3 tricks non-vulnerable, doubled (500 points)** and **2 tricks vulnerable, doubled (500 points)** if the opponents can make a vulnerable game for 620.

Another concept on judging hand value for a 3 level preempt is to consider the number of winners held. To ascertain winners, deduct the number of losers from 13:

- Deduct **1** winner for **each missing honor card** in the trump suit.
- Deduct **2** winners for a worthless **doubleton**.
- Deduct **1** for a **KQ** combination.
- Deduct **2** for a **QJ10** combination.

Six winners are needed when **non-vulnerable**, **seven** when **vulnerable**.

Consider Seating Position

Preempts in **first position** are the most **"normal" preempts**. In **third position**, the **standards may be relaxed**. Third hand may assume partner has 6-7 HCP's and actually incorporate those HCP's in his bid. Since third hand has that prerogative, his partner rarely raises. One should preempt in fourth position ONLY if he can make the contract in his own hand. Otherwise, pass it out and get some new "tickets".

The preempter has told his story. He doesn't bid again unless his partner makes a **forcing** call. **A simple raise is not forcing.** It is said that Charles Goren had a book in his library entitled "<u>Bids After You Have Preempted</u>." All of the pages were blank!

Three Level Preempts

Non-Vulnerable

S A Q 10 9 7 3 2	**S** 10 5	**S** 5 4
H J 10	**H** K Q 10 9 8 6 5	**H** K 3
D Q 6 5	**D** J	**D** Q J 10 9 8 7 6
C 10	**C** Q 5 4	**C** Q 10
Bid 3 spades	**Bid 3 hearts**	**Bid 3 diamonds**

Vulnerable

S A K J 10 9 8 6	**S** J 10	**S** 5 2
H 5 4	**H** A Q J 10 9 7 6	**H** Q J
D 10 9 8	**D** K 4	**D** 8 4
C Q	**C** 8 6	**C** K Q J 10 8 6 5
Bid 3 spades	**Bid 3 hearts**	**Bid 3 clubs**

Higher Level Preempts

4 Level	5 Level
S K Q J 10 9 6 5 2	**S** 9
H 4	**H** 3
D Q J 10	**D** K J 5
C 5	**C** K Q 10 9 7 6 5 4
Bid 4 spades	**Bid 5 clubs**

Weaker trump suits need compensating values in other suits.

Responding to Three-Level Preempts

Response to partner's preempt is based on the number of quick tricks held in the three unbid suits and/or voids and singletons. If opener uses the Rule of Two and Three, responder simply adds his quick tricks to the number of winners partner shows with his bid and responds accordingly. Since the opener has 7+ cards in the suit he bids, **quick tricks in the other three suits are of much more value than trump support. (Quick tricks: AK = 2, KQ = 1, QJ9 = ½ = approximately 15 HCP's.)** Responder should make every effort to raise partner as opposed to bidding a new suit.

A preemptive overcall is made by jumping the level of bidding after an opponent opens. (Opener 1 spade, his opponent 3 hearts). Responses are the same as if the preempt was made in first position.

Responder doesn't usually raise a third seat preempt. His partner will have assumed he has 6-7 HCP's. (This is often true on any third-seat opening bid.) Do not raise a fourth seat preempt except in competition.

We simply cannot make decisions as well when several rounds have been preempted as we can with low-level, routine bidding. Don't despair if early on you get in "too deep" – preempts usually pay off.

Partner Opens 3 Spades

S K Q 10 9	**S** Q J	**S** Q 2	**S** 5 2
H A K 10 5	**H** K J 10 9	**H** K J 10 9 8	**H** Q J 10 9
D K J 10	**D** A K 5	**D** 5	**D** K 10 9
C 10 9	**C** Q 10 9 8	**C** A K J 10 9	**C** A 10 9 8
Bid game	**Bid game**	**Bid game**	**Pass**

Putting it Together
Three Level Preempts

Opener	Responder	Meaning
3 H/S	4 of same suit	Sign off (can be obstructive or constructive)
3 H/S	3 NT	*Avoid
3 H	3 spades or 4 of a minor	**Forcing one round
3 S	4 C/D	Forcing one round
3 S	4 H	Sign Off
3 H/S	5 H/S	***Slam try
3 H/S	4 NT	Blackwood with support in partner's suit
3 C/D	3 H/S	**Forcing one round
3 C/D	4 C/D	Obstructive
3 C/D	5 C/D	Sign off
3 C/D	3 NT	Sign off
3 C/D	4 NT	Blackwood with support

   * Avoid responding 3 NT unless you have a source of your own and/or adequate cards to reach your partner's hand:

Partner 3 diamonds   You 3 NT – A 10 3 (diamonds)

   ** A change of suit by responder shows a very good 6-card suit with interest in a game in that suit. The opener raises with support, bids notrump or returns to his original suit. (He passes a game bid.)

*** A slam try in opener's suit.
- If opponents have bid, do you have first- or second-round control of that suit.
- If opponents have not bid, it asks about the quality of opener's trump suit **OR** the quality of the entire hand. Partners must agree!

When Opponents Interfere

- Responder may ignore interference and make the same call he would have made otherwise.
- A double of an interfering bid is for penalty.
- A notrump bid after interference shows stoppers in opponent's suit.

When Opponents Preempt

As stated earlier, the primary purpose of preempting is to interfere with opponents' bidding process. Don't fall for this if you have a hand worthy of competing. Listed below are some options:

- Holding an opening hand (13-16) and the right distribution, 4-4-4-1 or a similar distribution, double for takeout through 3 hearts. A double of a game is for penalty unless your partnership has agreed otherwise.
- Holding a strong suit with 13+ HCP's, overcall.
- Holding a strong suit and 19+, cue bid the opponent's suit to get partner's attention.
- Holding stopper(s) in opponent's suit and a notrump opener, bid 3NT.
- Holding a few high cards in opponent's suit and a good hand, pass and hope partner will make a balancing takeout double which you may choose to leave in for penalty.

Declarer South 4 Hearts
North-South Vulnerable
East-West Vulnerable

The Preemptive Bid

North (dealer)
S 6 2
H 8 6
D K Q 9 8 5 3 2
C A 7

West
S K J 8 7 5
H 5 4 3
D A
C 10 9 6 3

East
S Q 9 4 3
H 10
D J 7 6 4
C K J 5 4

South
S A 10
H A K Q J 9 7 2
D 10
C Q 8 2

The Bidding: North 3 diamonds – East pass – South 4 hearts – West pass, pass, pass.

The Lead: The 7 of spades

The Play and Defense: Win the Ace of spades, play the 10 of diamonds. Since West has the singleton Ace, he might cash the King of spades and lead a club as an **effort** to "kill" the dummy. If South is careful to watch his spots he might pick up the 10 of trumps and keep the 8 as an entry.

Tips: A preemptive bid usually has no defensive values. The hand should contain 2 of the top 4 honors in the suit bid, and the hand should <u>not</u> qualify for an opening bid on the one level.

A game bid after partner's preempt is to play.

Declarer West 5 Clubs
Both Vulnerable

The Preemptive Bid

North
S K Q J 4
H A 9 8 7
D K J 6
C 8 7

West (dealer)
S 3 2
H --
D Q 5 2
C A K Q 9 5 4 3 2

East
S 10 9 8 7
H J 10 6
D A 10 4 3
C J 10

South
S A 6 5
H K Q 5 4 3 2
D 9 8 7
C 6

The Bidding: West 5 clubs – North pass, pass, pass.

The Lead: The King of spades

The Play: West counts losers – 2 spades and 2 diamonds. His best bet to avoid 2 diamond losers is to play the 2 and insert the 10 if North plays low.

Tip: On the 5 level it's a little dangerous to double when it is unknown what cards East and partner hold. A double of 5 clubs is for penalty.

Declarer West 4 Spades
North-South Vulnerable

The Preemptive Bid

North (dealer)
S Q J
H J
D A 10 8 7 5
C A J 9 6 5

West
S A K 8 7 6 5 3 2
H 7
D 9 4 3
C K

East
S 9
H K Q 9 8 6 4
D K Q J 2
C 4 2

South
S 10 4
H A 10 5 3 2
D 6
C Q 10 8 7 3

The Bidding: North 1 diamond – East 1 heart – South pass – West 4 spades – North pass, pass, pass.

The Lead: The Jack of hearts

The Play: East plays the Queen, South wins and returns a the 10 of hearts (suit preference). West ruffs low, North overruffs and plays the Ace of diamonds – then the 5 of diamonds. South ruffs and plays another heart.

Tips: When a player jumps to game, even after his partner has made a call in another suit, he should have a 7- or 8-card suit and no support for partner's suit.

North-South has values for game in the club suit; but, since they are vulnerable, it is dangerous to bid at the 5 level after partner has passed.

Declarer West 4 Hearts
East-West Vulnerable

The Preemptive Bid

North
S 8 6 4
H 9 5
D 7 6 3
C K J 8 6 5

West
S 3 2
H A K J 10 8 7 4 3
D 4
C A 10

East
S Q 7 5
H Q 2
D A J 10 9 8 2
C 7 3

South (dealer)
S A K J 10 9
H 6
D K Q 5
C Q 9 4 2

The Bidding: South 1 spade – West 4 hearts – North pass, pass, pass.

The Lead: The 4 of spades

The Play: South wins the spade lead with the 9, plays the Ace, and then switches to a small club after observing his partner's discards.

Tip: The defensive team should determine to defeat the opponents on every hand if at all possible. Observing discards and count signals helps tremendously.

Declarer South 7 Spades
North-South Vulnerable

The Preemptive Bid

North
S A 4
H A 9 5 2
D A K Q 8 4 3
C A

West
S 9 5
H K 7
D 7 6 5 2
C 10 9 7 3 2

East (dealer)
S 10 8
H J 8 6 3
D J 10
C K Q J 6 5

South
S K Q J 7 6 3 2
H Q 10 5
D 9
C 8 4

The Bidding: East pass – South 3 spades – West pass – North 5NT* – East pass – South 7 spades – West pass, pass, pass.

The Lead: The 10 of clubs

The Play: Win the club, draw trumps and discard losers on the diamond suit.

Tip: When the preempter is vulnerable, he should be good for 7-8 tricks in his hand. Responder needs all of the other suits well protected and a good side suit to bid the Grand Slam Force.

* Grand Slam Force

106

Declarer West 5 Spades
North-South Vulnerable

The Preemptive Bid

North
S --
H 9
D A K Q 10 9 8 5 4
C Q 5 4 3

West
S A K 10 9 7 5 4
H 4
D 2
C A K J 2

East (dealer)
S Q 3 2
H A Q 7
D J 7 6
C 10 9 8 7

South
S J 8 6
H K J 10 8 6 5 3 2
D 3
C 6

The Bidding: East pass – South 4 hearts – West 4 spades – North 5 diamonds – East 5 spades – South pass, pass, pass.

The Lead: The Ace of diamonds, then the King

The Play: North wins the diamond Ace but West ruffs the King, draws trumps and finesses for the Queen of clubs which loses – making 5.

Tips: North-South were "bidding it up"; but, it didn't deter East from giving partner a raise above game level.

It is important to distinguish between a raise in competition and a raise with slam goals. All four players were "bidding blindly" but, that's what preempts are all about. The aggressive players usually come out better than timid players.

A game bid in a new suit after partner preempts is to play.

Declarer South 6 Spades
None Vulnerable

The Preemptive Bid

North
S K 2
H 7 5 3 2
D A K J
C A K 8 3

West
S --
H A K Q 9 8 4
D 9 8 7
C Q J 10 9

East (dealer)
S 10 8 5 3
H J 10 6
D 5 4 3
C 6 4 2

South
S A Q J 9 7 6 4
H --
D Q 10 6 2
C 7 5

The Bidding: East pass – South 3 spades – West 4 hearts – North 5 spades – East pass – *South 6 spades – West pass, pass, pass.

The Lead: The Ace of hearts

The Play: South ruffs the opening lead, draws trumps, plays the AKJ of diamonds and the AK of clubs, trumps a club to get back to his hand and claims.

Tip: *North's 5 spade jump bid asked South to bid 6 if he had first- or second-round control in hearts.

108

Declarer North 6 Hearts
North-South Vulnerable

The Preemptive Bid

<u>North</u>
S A
H Q J 9 7
D 10 2
C Q J 9 8 7 6

<u>West</u>
S 9 8 7 2
H 10 4 3 2
D A 9 8 7
C 5

<u>East</u> (dealer)
S K Q J 10 6 5 4
H 6
D J 4 3
C 4 3

<u>South</u>
S 3
H A K 8 5
D K Q 6 5
C A K 10 2

The Bidding: East 3 spades – South double – West 4 spades – North 5 hearts – East pass – South 6 hearts – West pass, pass, pass.

The Lead: The King of spades

The Play: North wins with the Ace of spades, draws 3 rounds of trumps – goes back to closed hand with a small club and leads a diamond toward dummy. West wins and leads another spade. Declarer ruffs the spade, draws West's last trump and runs the club suit, making 6.

Tips: North held longer clubs but gave preference to the major suit. When North responded 5 hearts over opponents intervening game bid, he showed HCP's and good hearts; therefore, South decided to go for a slam.

Declarer East 5 Diamonds
North-South Vulnerable

The Preemptive Bid

North
S J 6 4
H 6 2
D 5
C A K J 6 4 3 2

West
S A K Q 9
H A Q 9 5
D A Q 4
C 10 9

East (dealer)
S 10 7
H K 10
D K J 10 9 8 7 6
C Q 8

South
S 8 5 3 2
H J 8 7 4 3
D 3 2
C 7 5

The Bidding: East 3 diamonds – South pass – West 5 diamonds – North pass, pass, pass.

The Lead: The 8 of spades

The Play: Win the spade, draw trumps and discard club losers on the spade and heart suits.

Tip: East is non-vulnerable against vulnerable opponents, he hasn't much tolerance for the major suits. This is an excellent time to preempt.

Declarer North 3 NT
Both Vulnerable

The Preemptive Bid

North
S A 10 7
H A K 5 4
D 10 6 4
C K Q 8

West
S K J 8 5
H J 9 7 2
D A
C 10 9 6 3

East
S Q 9 4 3
H Q 10 3
D J 7
C J 5 4 2

South (dealer)
S 6 2
H 8 6
D K Q 9 8 5 3 2
C A 7

The Bidding: South 3 diamonds – West pass – North 3 NT, pass, pass, pass.

The Lead: The 3 of spades

The Play: Since South has only 1 stopper in the spade suit, he might as well win the first spade. He leads the 10 of diamonds and lets it ride if East doesn't cover.

Tips: A preemptive bid usually has no defensive values. The hand should contain 2 of the top 4 honors in the suit bid, and the hand should **not** qualify for an opening bid on the one level.

A preempt doesn't necessarily promise a solid suit nor an outside entry; therefore, the responder should usually have a minimum of 3 cards in his partner's suit to bid 3 NT. This is necessary to establish that suit and reach dummy. Declarer must also have all other suits protected.

WEAK-TWOS

The weak-two bids and the artificial two-club strong bids go hand in hand. The strong-2 opening bid of each suit is still played in some bridge groups; but recent beginning players and especially duplicate players strongly favor weak twos and the strong artificial 2-club opening bids. (The strong-2 bid is discussed separately.)

The weak-two bids are handled very much like the 3-level preempt and they serve the same purpose i.e., they interfere with opponents' bidding space (and sometimes partner's); they also suggest a lead if opponents win the bid. The guidelines are similar to 3-level preempts. The most obvious exception is that the **club suit is reserved for strong 2 opening bids** regardless of the suit expected to be the trump suit. Another exception is that responder may inquire about the quality of opener's hand by a bid of 2 NT – discussed under responses. A simple raise is obstructive and the opener should pass.

Avoid opening a weak-two major holding 4 cards in the other major unless partner is a passed hand. There may be game possibilities in that major which would be suppressed by a preempt.

Avoid opening a weak two with a void so that partner may correctly judge your hand value.

Many players will avoid the weak-two diamond bid because it reveals too much information. For this reason, some players prefer to use the two diamond call to show a 5-4 hand in the majors which is a conventional bid called "Flannery". (See Additional Popular Conventions, page 217.) The opponents are more likely to come into the bidding after a weak-two diamond bid than over a major-suit preempt. It is suggested the weak-two bidder should have some honor cards in the spade suit to open 2 diamonds – especially in third seat – as a deterrent to 4th seat.

Since the 2-diamond bid is often restricted and the 2-club bid is excluded, a player may **occasionally** open 3 clubs or 3 diamonds (usually after partner has passed) with a strong 6-card suit PROVIDED he holds compensating values. Those values might be an outside Ace or KQ combination, etc. The vulnerability should be favorable. Partner will pass if the opener is in third seat.

Below are some examples of hands that may be opened with a weak-two bid.

Non-Vulnerable

S	A J 10 7 6 5	S	5 4
H	K 4	H	K 3
D	5	D	K Q 10 9 6 5
C	8 7 6 5	C	7 6 4
Open 2 spades		**Open 2 diamonds**	

Vulnerable

S	A K J 9 6 5	S	8 7
H	Q 4	H	6 5
D	5 4	D	A K J 10 7 6
C	9 8 7	C	Q 4
Open 2 spades		**Open 2 diamonds**	

A hand containing 2 ½ quick tricks (A K 10 9 7 6 in one suit plus a K 3 in another suit) is too strong for a weak-two bid.

Summary
Guidelines for Opener

- **Six quality cards are needed.** If vulnerable, 3 of the top 5 honors are needed. If non-vulnerable, 2 of the top 5 are sufficient.

- The range of **pointcount** is wide. The bid shows from **5-11 HCP's** with most of the strength in the suit preempted. The hand does not contain an outside 4-card major unless partner is a passed hand.

- Requirements for opening in **third seat may be relaxed**. Opener may assume partner has some HCP's (7-8) when 2 people have passed.

- A **stronger hand** is needed in **fourth position**. Bid only what **your hand** will deliver.

- A very good 5-card suit or a weak 7-card suit may **occasionally** be opened in third position.

- To **overcall** with a weak-two bid, **skip one level** of bidding.

- **Avoid** opening the weak-two bid **with a void** so that partner can properly estimate your hand value.

Weak-Two Bids
Guidelines for Responder

The responder is responsible for deciding the final contract.

- A simple raise with equal vulnerability is preemptive; opener doesn't usually bid again.

- Non-vulnerable vs. vulnerable opponents, bid game with 3+ card support and a few side-suit winners. Just do it!

- A new suit response is suggested as a trump suit and is forcing one round:
  - Opener raises with support; otherwise, he returns to his suit or bids NT.

- R O N F, which is frequently shown on a convention card, is an acronym for "**raise** is the **only non-forcing call.**"
  - 2 H/S ↔ 3 H/S

- Responder may "carry on" with an intervening bid.

- A game bid in NT or any suit is to play.

On marginal game-going hands, responder may bid 2NT to ask opener for a valuable outside feature of his hand. The opener bids the suit containing the feature:

- 2 H/S ↔ 2 NT ↔ 3 clubs shows the Ace or protected King in that suit.

- 2 H/S ↔ 2 NT ↔ 3 NT shows a solid suit in hearts or spades. (A K Q 10 8 5).

- With no outside feature, opener rebids his suit at the three level.

- By **partnership agreement**, responder may bid 3 clubs (as opposed to 2 NT) to ask opener to show a side-suit singleton. This must be alerted.

  - 2 H/S ↔ 3 C ↔ 3 D shows a singleton diamond. Opener rebids his suit if he has no singleton. This eliminates the use of 3 clubs to show a real suit.

See "Additional Popular Conventions" page 217 for "Ogust," a more

definitive approach to responses after partner opens a weak-two.

Weak-Two Bids
Putting it together

Opener		**Responder**	
S	A J 10 7 6 5	S	Q 4
H	K 4	H	A J 9
D	5	D	K Q 7 6
C	8 7 6 5	C	A 9 4 3
2 spades		4 spades	
pass			

Opener		**Responder**	
S	A K J 9 6 5	S	Q 10 3
H	Q 4	H	J 10
D	5 4	D	A 5 3 2
C	9 8 7	C	K 6 5 4
2 spades		3 spades	
pass			

Opener		**Responder**	
S	K Q	S	A
H	10 9 3	H	K J 4
D	A 10 9 8 7 4	D	K Q J 3 2
C	10 8	C	K J 5 4
2 diamonds		2 NT	
3 spades		3 NT	
pass			

Declarer West 3 Spades
N-S Vulnerable

Weak Twos
Furthering the Preempt

North
S K
H Q 10 5 4
D A 8 5 2
C Q 9 5 3

West (dealer)
S Q J 8 7 6 5
H K 6
D 7 4 3
C 10 6

East
S A 9 4
H J 9 8 2
D Q 6
C K 8 7 2

South
S 10 3 2
H A 7 3
D K J 10 9
C A J 4

The Bidding: West 2 spades – North pass – East 3 spades – South pass, pass, pass.

The Lead: The 4 of hearts

The Play: West loses 2 diamonds, 2 clubs and 1 heart.

Tips: It is important for third hand to further the preempt to block South's opportunity to enter the bidding. He has too many losers to go on to game.

When responder makes a simple raise in the suit partner preempts, he is NOT looking for a game contract!

Declarer North 4 Spades
N-S Vulnerable

Weak Twos
Avoid a Ruff-Sluff

North (dealer)
S Q J 10 9 5
H --
D 3
C K 7 6 5 4 3 2

West
S A 3
H 8 7 6 5 3 2
D J 9 7 5
C A

East
S 4 2
H K Q J 10 9 4
D Q 4
C Q J 8

South
S K 8 7 6
H A
D A K 10 8 6 2
C 10 9

The Bidding: North pass – East 2 hearts – South double -- West 4 hearts – North 4 spades – East pass, pass, pass.

The Lead: The King of hearts

The Play: Declarer wins the Ace of hearts and plays a small spade toward the closed hand. West counts the hearts and should NOT lead another one when he wins the Ace of spades. He would give N-S a ruff-sluff – a no-no.

Tips: Preempts are meant to block opponents bidding space. Don't let it happen when holding good "tickets".

Bridge is a game of the majors. The double of one major promises the other one.

Declarer South 4 Hearts
None Vulnerable

Weak Twos
The 2 NT Inquiry

North
S A Q 9 5
H Q 10 8 3
D A 5
C J 10 9

West
S K J 7 4
H 9
D Q J 9 8 3
C K 7 4

East
S 6 3 2
H K 4
D 6 4
C A Q 8 5 3 2

South (dealer)
S 10 8
H A J 7 6 5 2
D K 10 7 2
C 6

The Bidding: South 2 hearts – West pass – North 2 NT – East pass – South 3 diamonds – West pass – North 4 hearts – East pass, pass, pass.

The Lead: The Queen of diamonds

The Play: Win the diamond in dummy, play the Queen of hearts. If East doesn't cover, the finesse can be repeated.

Tips: If unsure whether to pass or bid game, responder has a bid at his disposal to inquire about the quality of partner's preempt. A 2 NT call asks partner if he has an outside feature. If opener has no protected King or an Ace in a side suit, he repeats the suit he preempted.

North has an opening hand; but, he still has too many quick losers to bid game directly.

Declarer North 6 Clubs
E-W Vulnerable

Weak Twos
The Analytic Responder

North
S A J
H 8
D K 5
C A K Q 6 5 4 3 2

West
S Q 6 4 3 2
H 10 6 4
D Q 10 9 7
C 9

East
S K 8 7 5
H 5 3 2
D A J 6 4
C J 10

South (dealer)
S 10 9
H A K Q J 9 7
D 8 3 2
C 8 7

The Bidding: South 2 hearts – West pass – North 2 NT – East pass – South 3 NT – West pass – North 6 clubs – East pass, pass, pass.

The Lead: The Ace of diamonds

The Play: North made himself captain so the lead would come to his hand and the King of diamonds would be protected from a lead by West.

Tips: It is rare to change suits when partner has preempted. Bridge is not an exact science -- sometimes we simply must be aggressive, assertive and ambitious.

When responder bids 2 NT, he is asking opener to show a feature. South's 3 NT bid shows a solid suit. Responder most often raises partner's suit; he is not asking for a 3 NT contract. He has in mind a slam in clubs; but, he needs to learn more about partner's hand.

Declarer South 5 Diamonds, Doubled
E-W Vulnerable

Weak Twos
The Sacrifice Bid

North
S 7 6
H 8 6 4 3 2
D A 7 4 3
C K J

West
S A 10 9 8
H A Q 7
D 6 5
C A 10 5 4

East
S K Q 5 4
H K J 10 9
D 10
C Q 8 3 2

South (dealer)
S J 3 2
H 5
D K Q J 9 8 2
C 9 7 6

The Bidding: South 2 diamonds – West double – North 3 diamonds – East 4 diamonds – South pass – West 4 spades – North 5 diamonds – East pass, pass – West double – All pass.

The Lead: The Ace of clubs. East plays the 2. West switches to the Ace of spades – then the Ace of hearts. Bingo, East follows the heart lead with the Jack. East doesn't have a card 6 or above in spades that he can afford to play. West is looking to partner for some lead direction.

The Result: N-S loses 4 tricks. Down 2 doubled which equals a score of 300 for E-W as opposed to a score of 620 if E-W can make 4 spades, vulnerable.

Tips: When thinking of a sacrifice bid, the vulnerability is crucial. Decide how many tricks you may lose doubled; if it is less than opponents can make, just do it!

Did you recognize the cue bid? East's 4 diamond call tells partner he has game going values and asks partner to select the trump suit. East likes either major.

CHAPTER SEVEN: TWO SUITED OVERCALLS

THE UNUSUAL NOTRUMP

As you will recall, a 1 NT overcall shows a notrump opening hand with stoppers in opponent's opening suit. Systems are on – i.e., Stayman and the Jacoby Transfer. **To show a hand equivalent to a 2 NT opening bid after an opposing opening bid, the overcaller doubles first and then jump bids in notrump.** The 2 NT jump overcall is therefore available and is used for a two-suited takeout for the minors.

The unusual notrump call is made **over an opposing major suit opening bid by jumping a level of bidding:** Opponent 1 heart – You 2 NT – **shows a minimum of 5 cards in each minor**, AKA a two-suited hand.

Examples
2 NT Bidder's Hands

S K 5	**S** 5	**S** --
H 10	**H** 6 2	**H** 5 2
D A J 9 6 5	**D** A K J 10 9	**D** J 10 9 8 7 6
C K J 10 8 6	**C** K Q 10 8 7	**C** K J 10 9 8

As shown above, the unusual notrump **may be used with weak or strong hands**. The rebid after partner has chosen his best minor will relate to hand value and most importantly to vulnerability. It is often used as a non-vulnerable sacrifice bid against vulnerable opponents.

A rebid of 4NT by your partner after he has opened in first position and the opponent overcalls 4 hearts or 4 spades is also unusual for the minors.

The guidelines for responding to the unusual notrump for the minors are as follows:

- With 0-8 HCP's, make the lowest available call
- A jump bid under game is preemptive
- A jump to game may be preemptive or strong
- A cue bid of opponent's suit is forcing one round (A nice call when you can support either minor and have a nice hand)
- A new-suit bid (rare) is to play
- DO NOT pass – bid your longest minor even if it's only 1 card, unless opponent intervenes.

THE MICHAELS CUE BID

Michaels is another two-suited takeout. It shows **both majors**. Its distribution mirrors the unusual notrump distribution. When opponent opens 1 club or 1 diamond, **a cue bid of that suit shows 5 cards in each major suit** and asks you to bid your better of the two. An important difference is that unlike the unusual notrump, the Michaels bidder **does not jump bid; he simply bids the same suit as the opener.**

Opponent 1	You	Opponent 2	Your Partner
1 club / diamond	2 clubs / diamonds	pass	2 hearts or 2 spades

Example Hands for A Michaels Bid

S Q J 10 8 5 4	S A 10 9 7 6	S A K Q 10 5
H A 10 8 5 4	H K Q J 10 9	H K J 10 9 8
D --	D 8 7	D 9
C 5 4	C J	C J 5

The guidelines for responding to Michaels are as follows.

- With 0-8 HCP's, make the lowest available call
- A jump bid under game is preemptive
- A jump to game may be preemptive or strong
- A cue bid of opponent's suit is forcing one round (A nice call when you have equal suits and strength)
- A new-suit bid – a suit not shown by opener or partner is to play (rare)

Michaels and the Unusual Notrump may be used with weak or strong hands. **The overcaller shows his strength on the rebid.**

Michaels nor the Unusual Notrump need to be alerted; but, the opponent may request an explanation when it is his time to make a call. For a friendly atmosphere, you may announce **any** unusual call to unsuspecting opponents.

Some players use Michaels and the Unusual Notrump to show an unbid major and an unspecified minor. We suggest your partnership save "extensions" for later or never! If you "save for later", you may use the same guidelines for "regular" overcalls i.e., bid the higher ranking suit; and, if strong enough, bid the other on the next round of bidding.

An intervening call after Michaels or the Unusual Notrump doesn't prohibit partner answering; however, if responder passes and the two-suited overcaller bids, responder should correct to his longest suit. (Consider whether it is worth bidding to a higher level.)

Declarer East 6 Diamonds
None Vulnerable

The Unusual Notrump

North (dealer)
S A J 10 9 8 4
H A K 7 6 4
D 4 2
C --

West
S K 7
H --
D A K 10 7 6 5
C A K Q J 9

East
S 3 2
H J 9 8 2
D Q J 9 8
C 6 5 2

South
S Q 6 5
H Q 10 5 3
D 3
C 10 8 7 4 3

The Bidding: North 1 spade – East pass – South pass – West 2 NT – North 4 hearts – East pass – South pass – West 5 clubs – North pass – East 5 diamonds – South pass – West 6 diamonds – North pass, pass, pass.

The Lead: The 3 of hearts

The Play: East ruffs, draws trumps and plays the Ace of clubs. When North discards, declarer goes to the closed hand and finesses South for the 10 of clubs. He discards two spades on the club suit.

Tips: East's "spots" didn't change; his partner bid 5 clubs so that partner would pass with better clubs or bid diamonds with better diamonds.

Many players use the unusual notrump to show both minors. Some play it to show the two lower unbid suits. Discuss with partner.

Declarer West 4 Clubs
None Vulnerable

The Unusual Notrump

North (dealer)
S A Q J 9
H K Q J 5
D A 8
C Q 3 2

West
S 10 3 2
H A 8 7 6
D 4 2
C 10 8 7 6

East
S 8
H 3 2
D K Q J 7 6
C A K J 9 5

South
S K 7 6 5 4
H 10 9 4
D 10 9 5 3
C 4

The Bidding: North 1 club – East 2 NT – South pass – West 3 clubs – North double (takeout) – East pass – South 3 spades – West pass – North pass – East 4 clubs – South pass, pass, pass.

The Lead: The King of hearts

The Play: West wins the heart lead, plays a small club, inserts the Jack and plays the AK of clubs. He is "stuck" in the dummy so he plays the King of diamonds. North wins, takes a heart and the Ace of spades.

Tip: It is "unusual" to bid the Unusual NT after opponent opens one of the minors. Since East is sitting behind the clubs and has the perfect hand, he gives it a try. It is obvious North's HCP's are in the majors. Discuss with partners since one usually passes when opponent opens his best suit.

Declarer South 3 Spades, doubled
N-S Vulnerable

Michaels Cue bid

North
S K 10 9 5 4
H K Q J 10 9
D K
C Q 5

West (dealer)
S --
H A 2
D Q J 10 9 8 2
C A K J 8 6

East
S A Q 8 7 6
H 8 7 4
D A 5 4 3
C 10

South
S J 3 2
H 6 5 3
D 7 6
C 9 7 4 3 2

The Bidding: West 1 diamond – North 2 diamonds – East double (shows diamond support) – South pass – West 3 clubs – North double (takeout) – East redouble (10+ HCP's) – South 3 spades – West pass – North pass – East double (penalty) – South pass, pass, pass.

The Lead: The Ace of clubs, followed by the King and 6.

The Play: If declarer trumps with the 5, East overtrumps and plays the Ace of diamonds and then a small diamond to reduce declarer's trump holding. South isn't having fun!

Tip: Occasionally we must respect our partner's pass. North has a beautiful hand; but, his repeated takeout double was pushing his luck!

Declarer South 4 Spades
East-West Vulnerable

Michaels Cue bid

North
S Q J 10 9 8 4
H A K 5 4 3
D --
C 6 4

West (dealer)
S 3
H 9 8
D A Q 9 8 7
C A K J 10 9

East
S A 5
H Q J 7 6
D 10 6 5 4
C Q 8 5

South
S K 7 6 2
H 10 2
D K J 3 2
C 7 3 2

The Bidding: West 1 diamond – North 2 diamonds – East pass – South
2 spades – West 3 clubs – North 4 spades – East pass, pass, pass.

The Lead: The Ace and King of clubs

The Play: At least two hands are very distributional. Declarer might play to the
Ace and King of hearts, then trump a heart. He now ruffs a small diamond and
another heart.

Tip: You may use Michaels with a 6/5 hand in the majors – but **not** a 5/4.
Partner expects a minimum of 5. He may have to bid with only 2 or 3 cards in
the suit.

CHAPTER EIGHT: DOUBLES

When long-time bridge players think of doubles, they may only conjure up thoughts of the takeout or penalty double. Actually, there are several doubles that are absolutely essential for modern-day players. The **penalty double**, the **takeout double,** the **negative double** and the **lead-directing double** are discussed here in detail. Other less-used doubles are identified in the summary.

There is a practical method for determining the meaning of partner's double. **The double must be considered in the context of the bidding up to the time of the double.**

THE PENALTY DOUBLE

The **penalty double** is used as a method to exact a higher score by penalizing the opponents when they have overbid. If the opponents are defeated, the doubler's partnership gains a score of 100 per under trick with non-vulnerable opponents, 200 points per under trick if opponents are vulnerable. If the doubled partnership makes the contract, their score – doubled plus an insult penalty – goes in their plus column.

The context in which a penalty double is overcalled is most often when both partnerships have assets; but, one pair advances the bidding so high – the other stops bidding and pursues a score by doubling. The penalty double, formerly known as a business double, is most often imposed if and when one thinks the opponents can be **soundly** defeated. The doubler doesn't necessarily depend on his one or two good, long suits to defeat the opponent. He also needs tricks in declarer's suits – particularly in the trump suit.

Observe the hand below where EAST, non-vulnerable, will surely double for penalty against vulnerable opponents:

North (dealer)
S K Q 9 8 7 6
H 2
D A J 10
C Q J 9

West
S 2
H K 7 6 3
D 4 3 2
C 8 7 6 5 2

East
S A J 10
H A Q J 10 9
D K Q 5
C A K

South
S 5 4 3
H 8 5 4
D 9 8 7 6
C 10 4 3

The Bidding: North 1 spade – East double – South pass – West 2 hearts – North 3 spades – East double – South pass, pass, pass.

North should be soundly defeated. East -West should win 2 spades, 2 diamonds, 1 heart and 2 clubs – down 3.

The vulnerability and the doubler's position at the table play key roles in whether it is better to bid on or double for penalty as in the above hand where East – with a powerful hand (non-vulnerable) – plays after North (vulnerable).

The doubler's partner doesn't have to stand for a penalty double. He has the option of "pulling" the double by advancing the bidding. This is done more often because of weakness; BUT on some hands, the bidder may simply think

his team has the assets to make an even higher score by advancing the bidding.

The **partnership that has been doubled also has options** – each of

which is treacherous and is seldom used.

One of the partners may redouble which **by prior agreement** is a SOS call for rescue to another suit or notrump.

OR

By prior agreement, the redouble stands with the hope of making the contract.

The partnership must agree on which method to use.

The moral here is simple – don't grossly overbid when vulnerable AND

don't double for penalty when you think opponents have another suit available for

trumps. The latter "prior agreement" shown above will be used in examples in

this text.

The penalty double is usually imposed on high-level contracts – from

3 NT up and usually – but not always – when both partnerships have been vying

for the contract. A penalty double may be made against three-level contracts

even when your partnership has not entered the bidding. It is often obvious the

opponents have problems. It is usually a failure to find an early trump fit and/or

they are missing too many "biggies". Observe the following bidding:

Opponent 1	Partner	Opponent 2	You
1 club	pass	1 heart	pass
1 spade	pass	3 hearts	double

You hold:	**S** K Q 5
	H K 10 9 3
	D A 6 5
	C A J 10 9

The double is obviously for penalty. The opponents have a misfit. Partner should understand your double since you had a chance to double or overcall on the one level.

Another time a non-game contract may be doubled for penalty is when partner makes a takeout double and you have previously passed because the opponent has bid your best suit. The double may stand AND it is automatically converted to a penalty double. This is the main reason an opening bidder must do a re-opening double when his partner passes on the one level (partner 1 club – opponent 1 heart – you pass – opponent pass – partner double). This allows a penalty double to be imposed simply by passing.

Summary
The Penalty Double

- The double of all game contracts is for penalty unless a partnership has other conventional agreements.
- If you or your partner have previously made a penalty double by passing partner's takeout double, a double is for penalty.
- When you and your partner have each bid a different suit, a subsequent double is for penalty. (Don't confuse with a repeated takeout double where partner has not bid a suit.)
- If you or your partner has made a preemptive bid and second hand overcalls, a double by third hand is for penalty. (Partner 2 diamonds – Opponent 3 clubs – You double.)
- The double of an opponent's 1 or 2 NT opening bid (or 1 NT overcall) is for penalty.
- When you or your partner opens 1 or 2 NT and the next opponent overcalls, a double by third hand is for penalty.

THE TAKEOUT DOUBLE, REVISITED

You will recall that the **takeout double is used after the opponent has opened the bidding.** It shows 12+ HCP's in three unbid suits in second position. If each opponent has bid a different suit, the takeout double asks partner to choose between the two unbid suits. The takeout double is also used when a hand is too strong for an overcall (17+). The doubler's rebid will show his suit and his strength. The takeout is reviewed here to compare and contrast it with the penalty and negative doubles AND to emphasize three aspects which are often overlooked.

The **takeout double in the balancing position** allows one to enter the bidding when the bidding is dying at a low level. The "balancer" knows that the opponents aren't rich in HCP's; so, there is an "innate urge" to compete or push.

Partner	Opponent	You	Opponent
Pass	1 heart	pass	2 hearts
Pass	pass	double	pass
2 spades	pass	pass	pass

The **balancing takeout** may be made with less (9-10 HCP's) than is shown by a takeout in the first position (12+). The doubler may assume partner has some honor cards; he is actually bidding them with his takeout. Therefore, there is **no need to jump bid** even if holding 10+ HCP's. When both you and your partner have been silent during the first round of bidding and the **opponents have agreed on a low level suit contract**, a double by partner couldn't be for penalty. It is for takeout. Think "context" up to the time of the double. However, if either you or your partner passed for some "sly" reason – like a trap pass – then a correction is needed by that partner to show hand value after a balancing takeout double. (When an opponent opens the suit you were planning to open and you pass, you have made a trap pass.)

The **cue bid** is another call that is "under used" after partner has made a takeout double. **When partner doubles immediately after an opposing opening bid** and you hold a nice hand with nice honors (11-12 HCP's) – especially if holding a major – **the cue bid of the opponent's suit announces that you have the length and strength to go to game if partner's double is worth 13+ HCP's:** It says nothing about opponent's suit. The double of one major promises values in the other major.

Opponent 1	Partner	Opponent 2	You	Your Hand
1 heart	double	2 hearts	3 hearts	**S** K J 10 9
pass	3 or 4 spades	pass	pass	**H** 5
				D A Q 8 7
				C K J 10 9

The cue bid is especially helpful when the opponent opens a minor, partner doubles and you hold both majors. Partner could have a 5/4 hand in the majors, a 4/4 hand or even a 4/3 hand. This would allow him to choose his best major or notrump. **The double of a minor promises <u>both</u> majors..**

Opponent 1	Partner	Opponent 2	You	Your Hand
1 club	double	pass	2 clubs	**S** K 10 8 5
pass	2 H/S	pass	4 H/S	**H** A K 7 6
				D K 5
				C 10 9 8

REDOUBLE

The REDOUBLE by opponent after partner makes a takeout double is a call showing 10 + HCP's.

Opponent 1	Partner	Opponent 2	You
1 heart	double	redouble	be smart

If opponent 1 has 13+ HCP's and opponent 2 has 10+ HCP's as shown by his redouble – (usually the 10 HCP's held by opponent 2 is in a different suit than his partner's) – you may be in trouble. The opponents have the majority of the pointcount AND you <u>must</u> bid if you have a strong preference for a suit. Otherwise, opponent may be playing 1 heart, doubled – which is the equivalent of a two level bid (scorewise), redoubled is the equivalent of a 4-level bid. Partner will have another opportunity to bid; BUT, most of the time he **really needs to know your longest suit**. (If your suits are equal in length, you may pass and let partner choose his best suit.) Otherwise, the only time he wouldn't need to know your best suit is when he has 17+ and a self-sufficient suit. He will still have the opportunity to bid his suit if you make a bid; but, he may not have another opportunity to ask you to name your longest suit – so name it as if you have the best hand at the table. Don't let a hesitating sigh help the opponent!

If a redouble shows 10+ HCP's, a bid after a takeout double shows less than 10. (It is still forcing for one round.) Discuss these bids with partners and bridge clubs. Learning new tricks alone is not very fruitful!!

THE NEGATIVE DOUBLE

As with most bidding sequences, the negative double revolves around finding a 4-4 fit in a major suit. The negative double is a takeout for partner to bid; but, the context in which it is used is different from the classic takeout. **The negative double is used after partner has opened and right-hand opponent has overcalled.**

The negative double is usually used through 2 spades; however, it may be used on higher bidding levels by agreement with partners. **The double is a request for partner to bid the suit which your double promises.** You have sufficient HCP's to compete for a contract; but due to the limitations placed for card length and/or HCP's after an intervening overcall, you cannot bid your major as shown below:

Partner	Opponent 1	Your Call	Your Hand
1 club	1 spade	double	**S** 10 9
			H A K 10 9
			D J 6 5 2
			C 10 9 8

You would be showing 5 hearts and 10 HCP's if you
bid the heart suit. If partner doesn't have 4 hearts,
he selects another suit.

The following table shows other bids available when using the negative double. The pointcount needed depends upon the level of the contract. There is no upper limit on HCP's. The number in parentheses suggests a minimum pointcount needed to use the negative double as shown in the examples.

Listed below are examples of how to use the negative double after partner opens and there is an immediate overcall by opponent.

	Partner	Opponent 1	You	Your Hand
(1)	1 spade	2 clubs	double	**S** 10 5
				H A K 10 9
				D 8 7 6 4
				C A 8 5
	A bid of two hearts would show 5 hearts (8+ HCP's).			
(2)	1 spade	2 clubs	double	**S** 10 5
				H 9 8 7 6 5
				D A 10 9 4
				C Q J
	You have 5 hearts but not enough HCP's to bid on the 2 level (8+ HCP's).			
(3)	1 club	1 diamond	double	**S** A Q 9 5
				H 10 9 8 7
				D J 2
				C K 8 5
	You must have both majors. This is the only bidding sequence that promises both majors (6+ HCP's).			
(4)	1 diamond	2 clubs	double	**S** 10 9 4
				H K Q J 10
				D Q J 5 4
				C 7 6
	You promise only 1 major after this sequence. Therefore you need diamond support in case partner has neither or the wrong major (8+ HCP's).			
(5)	1 diamond	1 heart	double	**S** A J 10 4
				H 8 7
				D K J 8 2
				C 6 5 4
	Your double shows 4 spades (8+ HCP's). A bid of 1 spade would show 5 cards in the spade suit since one major has been bid.			
(6)	1 spade	2 hearts	double	**S** J 5
				H 5 4 3
				D A 9 8 7
				C K Q J 10
	If both major suits have been bid, a double shows both minor suits with a minimum of 4 cards in each or a long minor which you may rebid as a sign-off.			

Summary
The Negative Double

If partner's rebid will be on the one level (1 club –
1 diamond – you double) a minimum of 6 HCP's is needed
and always a minimum of 4 cards.

If his rebid will be on the two level (1 heart –
1 spade – you double), 7-8 HCP's are needed.

If his rebid will be on the three level (1 spade –
2 hearts – you double), 10 HCP's are needed and a
minimum of 4 cards in each minor.

The Opener's Rebid

---

* With a minimum (13-16), he makes the cheapest bid available.

* With a medium hand (17-18), he may jump a level in
  previously bid suit or bid another suit. Invitational.

* With a maximum-strength hand (19-21), he gets the
  partnership to game. If unsure about the suit or notrump, he
  will cue bid opponent's suit so that responder may clarify his
  holdings. The cue bid is the only game-force call.

The Responder's Rebid

---

* With 10 HCP's or less, he may give a simple preference for
  opener's suit or bid his suit at the lowest level – non-forcing.

* With 11-12, responder may raise opener's second bid, give a
  jump preference of opener's first suit, or bid 2 NT – all
  invitational.

* The cue bid of opponent's suit is the only game-force bid.
  The cue bid shows 12+. (If responder knows where the
  contract should be, he puts it there!).

The following chart is from one of Marty Bergen's great books, <u>Points Schmoints</u>

<u>Series: Negative Doubles.</u> It is filled with extensive information.

Comparing Negative and Takeout Doubles	
Negative Double	**Takeout Double**
Partner opened	An opponent opened
The double is made by the responder	The double is made by the overcalling side
Overcaller's suit is doubled	Opener's suit is doubled
6+ HCP's are needed at the one level, more at higher levels	11+ HCP's are needed at the one level, more at higher levels
Emphasis is on the unbid major(s)	All unbid suits are promised
You need not be short in the opponent's suit	You must be short in the opponent's suit
A negative double followed by a bid in a new suit is weak	A takeout double followed by a bid in a new suit is strong (17+ HCP's)

LEAD DIRECTING DOUBLES

The double of all artificial bids is lead directing. The bid of an artificial suit, by nature, infers the bidder's interest lies in another suit.

The **lower** on the bidding ladder the artificial call is made, the **more** cards are needed in the suit doubled. This will **avoid** the opponents playing a low-level doubled – and perhaps redoubled – contract. The Stayman 2-club call and 2-diamond responses are good examples of low level doubles. Lesser cards (AQJ, KQ10) will suffice on high-level doubles – Gerber and Blackwood, for example. You know opponents must bid again. Some examples:

- Stayman – 2 clubs and 2 diamond response
- Jacoby Transfer – 2 diamonds, hearts or spades
- Blackwood responses – clubs, diamonds, hearts or spades
- Gerber – 4 clubs and responses
- Cue bids
- Splinter bids

Summary
Doubles

Penalty double	↔	to exact a higher score when **opponents** have **overbid**.
Takeout double	↔	to ask partner to select a suit **after opponents** have **opened**.
Balancing takeout	↔	to ask partner to bid his best suit **when opponents have found a low-level fit**. (You and partner have previously passed.)
Negative double	↔	asks partner to select another suit **after** an **overcall** by next opponent.
Lead directing	↔	asks partner to lead a particular suit.
Reopening double	↔	asks partner to bid after you have opened, opponent overcalls and partner has passed.

Declarer West 4 hearts
Both Vulnerable

Doubles
Negative

North
S A K J 10 2
H J 9 5 2
D 7
C K 6 3

West (dealer)
S Q 5 4
H A Q 8 4
D A K 10 5 3
C 9

East
S 8 7 6
H K 10 7 3
D Q 6 2
C A Q 10

South
S 9 3
H 6
D J 9 8 4
C J 8 7 5 4 2

The Bidding: West 1 diamond – North 1 spade – East double – South pass – West 3 hearts (18 counting singleton) – North pass – East 4 hearts – South pass, pass, pass.

The Lead: The Ace of spades, followed by the King

The Play: After South's high-low on the spade leads, North plays another spade for partner to ruff.

Tips: East has enough HCP's to make a free bid – BUT he has only 4 hearts. Without the use of the negative double, E-W would not know they had a 4-4 fit in a major. It takes 5 hearts and 10 HCP's to bid hearts after opponent overcalls 1 spade.

The reverse bid doesn't apply after partner has used the negative double.

Declarer South 1 spade, doubled
East-West Vulnerable

Doubles
The Reopening Double
The Double for Penalty

North
S --
H Q J 9 8
D 10 8 7 6 4 3
C Q 6 5

West
S K Q J 10 8 4
H 6 5 2
D A
C J 10 4

East (dealer)
S 3
H A 7 4 3
D K J 9 2
C A K 3 2

South
S A 9 7 6 5 2
H K 10
D Q 5
C 9 8 7

The Bidding: East 1 diamond – South 1 spade – West pass -- North pass – East double – South pass, pass, pass.

The Lead: The Ace of diamonds, then the Jack of clubs. East wins and plays the King of diamonds – West discards a small heart – East returns another diamond for West to ruff – East wins another club and gives West still another ruff AND the party has just begun!

Tips: It is <u>very</u> <u>important</u> for the opening bidder to make a reopening double when there is a simple overcall followed by two passes – ESPECIALLY if he is short in the suit overcalled.

The opener's double after opponent's overcall is for takeout. West loved the <u>reopening</u> <u>double</u> which gave him the opportunity to impose a <u>penalty</u> <u>double</u> simply by passing. If West doubled the first time, his partner would think negative.

East should win the first club with the King (if North covers) so partner will know he also has the Ace.

Declarer North 3NT, doubled
Both Vulnerable

Doubles
Lead Directing

North (dealer)
S K 6
H 5 4
D A K Q 9 8 2
C Q 7 3

West
S A J 8
H A Q 10 9 7
D 3
C K 9 6 2

East
S 10 9 5 2
H 3 2
D J 10 7 6 4
C 5 4

South
S Q 7 4 3
H K J 8 6
D 5
C A J 10 8

The Bidding: North 1 diamond – East pass – South 1 heart – West pass – North 3 diamonds – East pass – South 3 spades – West pass – North 3 NT – East pass, pass, West double.

The Lead: The 3 of hearts

The Play: West wins the heart lead and plays the Ace and another heart. South may attempt to develop another entry to dummy before trying to run the diamond suit. If it's a small lead to the Queen of clubs, West wins the King and plays another heart. Meanwhile, East MUST hold on to every diamond card in order to stop that suit.

Tips: The double of a freely bid (no interference) notrump contract calls for the first-bid suit of dummy.

Third hand should **always** try to keep parity with "important" cards in the dummy.

Declarer South 4 spades
None Vulnerable

Doubles
The Cue Bid

North (dealer)
S K 6 2
H A Q 3
D K J 10 9 8 7
C 6

West
S J 7
H J 6 2
D Q 4 3 2
C 8 5 4 3

East
S 5 4 3
H 7 5 4
D A
C K Q J 10 9 2

South
S A Q 10 9 8
H K 10 9 8
D 6 5
C A 7

The Bidding: North 1 diamond – East 2 clubs – South 3 clubs – West pass – North 3 diamonds – East pass – South 3 spades – West pass – North 4 spades – East pass, pass, pass.

The Lead: The 3 of clubs

The Play: Declarer wins the club lead, trumps a club and draws trumps. The rest is easy.

Tip: When either partner cue bids as in the above bidding sequence, he has made a forcing bid to elicit more information from partner. The club bid says nothing about the quality of his club suit.

Declarer North 4 hearts
None Vulnerable

Doubles
The Negative Double

North (dealer)
S K 6 2
H A Q 3 2
D 2
C K Q 10 9 6

West
S Q 7 5 4
H J 6
D Q 4 3
C 5 4 3 2

East
S 8 3
H 7 5 4
D A K J 10 9 8 7
C A

South
S A J 10 9
H K 10 9 8
D 6 5
C J 8 7

The Bidding: North 1 club – East 1 diamond – South double – West pass – North 3 hearts – East pass – South 4 hearts – West pass, pass, pass.

The Lead: The Ace of diamonds, then the King

The Play: Declarer ruffs the King of diamonds, draws trumps and plays a club to establish that suit.

Tips: The above bidding sequence (opener 1 club, overcaller 1 diamond) is the only time the negative doubler **absolutely holds both majors**. Why? If he had only 1, he could bid it on the one level – even with only 4 cards.

146

Declarer East 3NT
Both Vulnerable

Doubles
The Redouble

North
S K Q J 4
H A 9 8 7
D J 6 4 2
C 8

West (dealer)
S 3 2
H 2
D K Q 5
C A K J 9 5 4 3

East
S A 10 9 8
H Q J 10
D A 10 3
C Q 7 2

South
S 7 6 5
H K 6 5 4 3
D 9 8 7
C 10 6

The Bidding: West 1 club – North double – East redouble – South 2 hearts – West 3 clubs – North pass – East 3NT – South pass, pass, pass.

The Lead: The 4 of hearts

The Play: East counts winners and has no trouble making the contract. He is in with the third heart lead and can put the losing spades on the long club suit.

Tips: When East redoubled, he was announcing the hand belonged to E-W.

South needs to bid even with 3 HCP's – otherwise, West will pass and North will have to guess South's longest suit. South's bid promises NUTTIN but a preference for hearts. How could he have much?

Declarer North 3NT
North-South Vulnerable

Doubles
The Redouble

North (dealer)
S K J 10 8 5
H A 3
D Q 8 7
C Q J 3

West
S 9 7 6 4 3 2
H 2
D 5 4 3 2
C 10 8

East
S Q
H K 10 6 5
D A J 10 6
C A 9 7 5

South
S A
H Q J 9 8 7 4
D K 9
C K 6 4 2

The Bidding: North 1 spade – East double – South redouble – West
2 diamonds – North pass – East pass – South 3 hearts – West pass – North
3 NT – East pass, pass, pass.

The Lead: The Jack of diamonds

The Play: Declarer wins the King in dummy, unblocks the Ace of spades, plays
a small heart to the Ace, discards a couple of dummy's clubs on the spade suit
and plays a small heart toward dummy.

Tips: When partner redoubles a takeout double, he is usually saying "partner I
have 10 or more HCP's" and no fit with your bid. He is "thinking" the opponent
may be in trouble." Discuss with partners and/or bridge clubs exactly what a
redouble means within your partnership.

   If West bids, North may pass the bidding back to his partner to hear what
he wants to say.

Declarer West 5 spades, doubled
Both Vulnerable

Doubles
Penalty

North (dealer)
S --
H 7 2
D A J 10 8 7 6
C A Q J 9 6

West
S A K 8 7 6 5 3
H --
D 9 5 4 3
C K 5

East
S 9 2
H K Q 9 6 5 4
D K Q 2
C 4 2

South
S Q J 10 4
H A J 10 8 3
D --
C 10 8 7 3

The Bidding: North 1 diamond – East 1 heart – South pass – West 4 spades – North 5 clubs – East 5 spades – South double – West pass, pass, pass.

The Lead: The Ace of diamonds

The Play: South discards the 3 of clubs – North plays the Jack of diamonds – East the Queen and South ruffs. South leads a club – North wins, plays another diamond for partner to ruff, etc.

Tips: When you want partner to stop bidding because you have opponents' trumps, and/or no support for partner – double for penalty ASAP.

Any time the opponent is bidding "your suit" – pass and await developments.

Declarer West 4 clubs
North-South Vulnerable

Doubles
The Takeout

North (dealer)
S K 4 3
H A K Q 9 4 2
D 8 4
C A 7

West
S 10 9
H J 10 8 5
D 6 5 3
C Q J 9 8

East
S A Q J 8
H 3
D K Q J 9
C K 10 6 2

South
S 7 6 5 2
H 7 6
D A 10 7 2
C 5 4 3

The Bidding: North 1 heart – East double – South pass – West 2 clubs – North 3 hearts – East 4 clubs – South pass, pass, pass.

The Lead: The Ace of hearts

The Play: Declarer wins the second heart with the 10 of clubs in dummy – plays the 2 toward closed hand. If North doesn't take the Ace, declarer might play the 10 of spades and let it ride.

Tips: East's hand is the most ordinary shape for a takeout double.

When declarer is trumping a trick in front of next player, he doesn't "send a boy to do a man's work." He trumps high enough not to be overtrumped, especially when he holds equal honors in the other hand.

Declarer South 2 hearts
Both Vulnerable

Doubles
Bidding a Weak Hand
after using the Negative Double

North (dealer)
S 7 4 2
H 3 2
D A K Q 8
C A K 6 2

West
S K 9
H Q 6 4
D J 9 6 5
C Q 8 7 5

East
S A Q 10 6 5
H A 5
D 10 7 3
C 10 9 3

South
S J 8 3
H K J 10 9 8 7
D 4 2
C J 4

The Bidding: North 1 diamond – East 1 spade – South double – West pass – North 2 clubs – East pass – South 2 hearts – West pass, pass, pass.

The Lead: The King of spades

The Play: South loses the first 4 tricks to the spade suit and a spade ruff. He will also lose the Ace of hearts – but, will eventually make his contract.

Tips: North will know South has a long heart suit but a weak hand when partner (South) uses the negative double and then bids his suit. If he had 10 points, he would bid instead of using the negative double.

Declarer South 4 spades
North-South Vulnerable

Doubles
Takeout

North
S K J 4
H 9 8 2
D 10 4 2
C Q J 8 6

West (dealer)
S 8 7 5
H 6 4
D 9 8 6 5 3
C 9 4 2

East
S 6 2
H A K Q 7 5 3
D Q
C K 10 7 3

South
S A Q 10 9 3
H J 10
D A K J 7
C A 5

The Bidding: West pass – North pass – East 1 heart – South double – West pass – North 2 clubs – East 3 hearts – South 3 spades – West pass – North 4 spades – East pass, pass, pass.

The Lead: The 6 of hearts

The Play: South wins the third lead with a high spade, leads a small trump to dummy and plays the Queen of clubs if East doesn't cover. (He should since he holds the 10).

Tips: South's double followed by a bid shows a hand value of 17+ points and a good suit. This kind of takeout is used when you could overcall – BUT how would you let partner know you are "loaded"??

Declarer East 3 hearts
East-West Vulnerable

Doubles
Negative

North
S 6 3 2
H Q 8
D K 9 8 7 6
C 4 3 2

West
S A 7
H A 6 5 4
D 10 5 4
C K 9 8 7

East (dealer)
S K 8 5
H J 10 9 7
D Q 2
C A Q J 6

South
S Q J 10 9 4
H K 3 2
D A J 3
C 10 5

The Bidding: East 1 club – South 1 spade – West double – North pass – East 2 hearts – South pass – West 3 hearts -- North pass, pass, pass.

The Lead: The Queen of spades

Tips: The opening bidder assumes his partner – the negative doubler – has less than 10 HCP's until he hears from partner again. With a minimum hand (13-16) the opener makes a minimum rebid. The negative doubler now passes with a minimum, invites with 10-11 – goes to game with 12+.

Unless the opener and overcaller each bid a major, the negative doubler will ALWAYS have one major.

Declarer North 4 spades
North-South Vulnerable

Doubles
after Stayman
The Double of Artificial Bids is
Lead Directing

North
S A 10 8 7 6
H K 9 8 7
D 5 4
C A 4

West
S J 9 3
H 10 6 5
D 8 7 3
C 9 8 7 6

East
S Q 2
H 4 3 2
D Q J 6
C K Q J 10 2

South (dealer)
S K 5 4
H A Q J
D A K 10 9 2
C 5 3

The Bidding: South 1 NT – West pass – North 2 clubs – East double – South 2 diamonds – West pass – North 3 spades – East pass – South 4 spades – West pass, pass, pass.

The Lead: The King of clubs

Tips: As long as responder holds 1 4-card major, he may use Stayman. If he holds both majors and one is longer, his rebid denotes the length and strength of his hand. With a minimum of 10 HCP's, he must jump on the rebid to force opener to game. If opener held only 2 spades, his rebid would be 3NT.

East's double of 2 clubs shows a decent club suit and asks partner to lead a club. (He didn't know he would be on lead.) The reason East must have a pretty good suit is because the opponents could otherwise decide to play clubs doubled.

Declarer South 2 spades
None Vulnerable

Doubles
The Balancing Takeout Double
when Partnership has Passed

<u>**North**</u> (dealer)
S A 10 8 4
H 8 6 5
D 9 8 2
C A K 6

<u>**West**</u>
S 9 5
H J 10 9
D K Q 5 4
C J 9 8 7

<u>**East**</u>
S K 7 3
H A K Q 7 2
D 10 7
C 5 4 3

<u>**South**</u>
S Q J 6 2
H 4 3
D A J 6 3
C Q 10 2

<u>**The Bidding:**</u> North pass – East 1 heart – South pass – West 2 hearts – North double – East pass – South 2 spades – West pass, pass, pass.

<u>**The Lead:**</u> The Jack of hearts

<u>**Tip:**</u> The balancing takeout is made when the opponents' bidding seems weak and/or they have found a low-level fit. The doubler assumes partner holds HCP's and thus can balance with 3-4 HCP's less than a classic takeout double. For this reason responder **DOES NOT jump the level with his response when both hands have passed.** (See next hand.)

*Note: North is a passed hand.

Declarer South 2 spades
None Vulnerable

Doubles
The Balancing Double
when Fourth Hand has Not Passed

North
S K J 10
H 5 3 2
D A 6 5
C Q J 6 5

West
S 9 7 2
H 8 7 6
D J 8 7
C A 10 9 8

East (dealer)
S 8 5 4
H A K Q J 10
D K 9 2
C 7 4

South
S A Q 6 3
H 9 4
D Q 10 4 3
C K 3 2

The Bidding: East 1 heart – South pass – West pass – North double – East pass – South 2 spades – West pass, pass, pass.

The Lead: The 8 of hearts

Tips: Unless North enters the bidding, it will die. There is **very rarely** a reason to allow opponents to play on the one level. North doesn't have an ideal takeout, but he has SPADES which his double shows. There are 40 HCP's divided among the four hands. East has less than 22 and West has less than 6. Since it is known that his partner holds values, North is **bidding both hands**; however, his partner doesn't know North's hand so **he jumps if he has 10+ and a nice 4-card suit**. A 4-3 fit often plays well, especially on the two level. (See previous hand).

The lead of the 8 tends to deny an honor card.

Declarer South 6 spades, doubled
None Vulnerable

Doubles
The Lightner Slam
Lead-Directing Double

North (dealer)
S A 10 9 6
H 7 3
D K J
C A Q 10 6 2

West
S --
H J 10 9 4
D Q 10 5
C J 9 8 5 4 3

East
S 7 4 2
H A K 8 6 5 2
D 9 7 3 2
C --

South
S K Q J 8 5 3
H Q
D A 8 6 4
C K 7

The Bidding: North 1 club – East 2 hearts – South 2 spades – West 4 hearts – North 4 spades – East pass – South 4 NT – West pass – North 5 hearts – East pass – South 6 spades – West pass – North pass – East double – South pass, pass, pass.

The Lead: The five of clubs

Tips: The Lightner Slam Double calls for an unusual lead: NOT a suit bid by your partnership, NEVER a trump.

The partner who doubles expects his partner to decide the correct suit to lead. On the above hand, it is more obvious than usual with 6 cards in the club suit which was bid by the opponent.

Declarer South 3 NT, doubled
None Vulnerable

Doubles
Lead-Directing

North (dealer)
S A 4
H K Q 10
D 10 9 2
C K 10 9 8 7

West
S 7 6 3
H 6 5 4 3
D A K 4 3
C 5 2

East
S J 10 9 8 2
H J 8 7
D J 2
C A Q J

South
S K Q 5
H A 9 8
D Q 8 7 6 5
C 4 3

The Bidding: North 1 club – East pass – South 2 NT – West pass – North 3 NT – East double – South pass, pass, pass.

The Lead: The King of diamonds, then the 5 of clubs

The Play: East wins the club lead and returns the Jack of diamonds to the Ace. West returns another club. East cashes his two winners and returns the 2 of diamonds to defeat the contract.

Tips: The double of an uncontested notrump contract (3NT or a slam) calls for the first-bid suit of dummy.

Defense is just as much fun as declarer play when one takes advantage of the available gadgets. When West led the King of diamonds and it held, East knew how to hit partner again allowing him to stay over dummy.

CHAPTER NINE: THE PLAY OF THE HAND

Before declarer begins playing a hand – before he calls for a card in dummy – **he needs a standard plan** of action. Someone has suggested declarer shouldn't play to the first trick until he has considered what he will do on the second trick. A good player will determine a goal and formulate a standard plan of action – then incorporate all additional bits of information into his plan as the play progresses.

A R C H
A Plan to Consider

Consider ARCH, an acronym for **analyze the lead**, **review the bidding**, **count losers/winners** and "H" represents **how to put it together**.

The objective of a plan – in addition to "savoring" the sheer joy of playing – is to make the number of tricks for which you have contracted. It is an added joy to make overtricks. Taking every trick that isn't "nailed down" improves playing ability and greatly impresses partner. Don't be concerned when it is necessary to relinquish the lead. It must happen to fulfill your goal unless you've bid a grand!

Analyze the Lead
Review the Bidding

If opponents have opened or overcalled during the bidding process, the declarer gets an informative "peek" into their hands. The bidding will give information on opponents' holding – on the **strength and length** of the suit(s) named and thus allow declarer to begin **getting a count** on opponents' holdings.

The lead – whether or not there have been interfering bids – tells a "story" which must be heard. For instance, the lead of the Jack promises the 10 and 9 (8) pinpointing invaluable **key spot cards**. The Lead Table in the next chapter is applicable on all leads including return (second) leads; however, there are helpful observations one should note about opponent's hand gleaned from the lead:

Suit Contracts

- If an opponent has overcalled and is on lead but doesn't lead the suit he bid, assume he has a combination from which he chooses not to lead (AQ, KJ).

- If overcaller's partner is on lead, his leads are also standard (A̲xx, Q6̲2, K̲Q).

- If an opponent leads the Ace, he usually has the King, if he leads the King, he has the Queen, etc. Thus stated, if he leads the Jack, he denies holding the Queen.

- If he leads 4th card down, he may have only one honor card in that suit.

- If he leads a suit strongly bid by opponents, it will usually be a singleton.

- If neither opponent entered the bidding and you're missing a few "biggies" assume the honor cards are divided between the opponents' hands. WATCH SIGNALS to learn about opponents' distribution!

Notrump Contracts

- If opponent leads an honor, it will be the top of a sequence or from 2 if his partner has bid the suit.

- If his lead is under a 6, he will usually have an honor card.

- If his lead is above a 6, it may be the top of nothing.

Count

One author stated that "all one had to do to be a bridge player was to learn to count to 13." Counting is a vital part of bridge whether bidding, playing or defending.

Count Losers in a Suit Contract
Count Winners in a Notrump Contract

As declarer in a suit contract, count as **quick losers** every card **that isn't** an Ace, AK, AKQ or AKQJ in combination of both hands.

As declarer in a **notrump** contract **count** all of the above honor cards as winners – add to them any sequential spot cards (A K Q J <u>10</u> <u>9</u>).

Examples of Counting
Losers and Winners

Declarer's Hand			Declarer's Hand	
Suit Contract	Losers		Notrump Contract	Winners
S A Q 9 8	1		**S** Q J 10 4	1
H K J 10 9 8	1		**H** A K 5	2
D A J	0		**D** A 10	2
C A J	4		**C** Q J 10 9	0
Partner's Hand			Partner's Hand	
S K 7 6			**S** A 6 5	
H A 5 4			**H** J 10 9	
D K 9			**D** K 9	
C 10 9 8 7 6			**C** K 8 7 6 4	

Keep in mind these are **quick winners and losers**. There are rarely hands in which suits don't need to be established. They may be established by different methods of play.

How to Put It Together

After analyzing, reviewing and counting comes the HOW! The development of the play proceeds by side-suit establishment, trumping losers in dummy, drawing trumps, finessing, end playing the opponent, etc. The order in which each play is executed depends upon the "urgency" of maintaining control over losers and the trump suit. The timing of plays is of utmost importance on each hand.

When to Delay Drawing Trumps

Foremost in any declarer plan of suit play is recognizing when to draw trumps. Unless there is a good reason to postpone drawing trumps, **do so very early** in the play to avoid opponents ruffing in. Perhaps this can more easily be remembered by concentrating on specific times when it is **necessary to make other plays before drawing trumps**.

- When declarer needs to trump losers contained in the closed hand with dummy's trumps
- When the high trump honor cards are held by opponents and the dummy has a solid suit on which to discard losers
- When dummy's trumps are needed for transportation
- When declarer needs to crossruff a hand

Maintaining Control of the Trump Suit

It is very important that declarer maintain control of the trump suit.

To trump in the closed hand and shorten the trump suit could give control of the hand to opponents. Do most of the trumping in dummy. When trumps are badly

162

divided, consider a loser on loser play, a safety play and/or continually running an established suit until opponents ruff in. Another possibility is to eliminate side suits and throw opponent on lead with a small trump so that he must lead into your hand.

THE END PLAY

An **end play** may be defined as a play by declarer that forces his opponent to make a play which presents him with a trick that otherwise may not be available to him.

Mrs. Dorothy Hayden Truscott[1] quotes a famous player as having summed up the difference between an average player and an expert as follows:

> The average player knows **how** to finesse.
> The expert knows **how not** to finesse.

Mrs. Truscott gave the following layout to illustrate an **end play:**

```
                        North
                        S A Q 2
West                                        East
S J 8 7                                     S K 9
                                            H A
                        South (declarer)
                        S 4 3
                        H K
```

Declarer eliminated all suits in hands to the cards shown. When declarer leads the King of hearts, East must win and return a spade into the A Q.

---

[1] Dorothy Hayden Truscott, <u>Winning Declarer Play</u>

Mrs. Truscott suggests that one must first learn how to finesse properly and then try the end plays. She suggests further one must also have digested the long-hand, short-hand principle as shown below:

- Draw trumps in the long hand
- Ruff losers in the short hand
- Ruff in the closed hand **only** when trumps are plentiful

THE FINESSE

The **finesse** may be defined as an effort by declarer to win a trick with a card smaller than one held by an opponent by playing after the opponent. The need to finesse is common on almost every hand. The end play is less available because the ability to eliminate all suits is not always possible.

According to an ACBL publication, how one executes a finesse **depends upon the number of tricks declarer needs from a particular suit.** The publication showed numerous card combinations that "crop up" in every game.

With two suits in which a finesse is necessary, work on the suit that is unevenly divided first. If you have the A Q of a suit in one hand and the 10 6 in the other, you will have established one extra trick with a successful finesse. If you have a 5/2 suit, you can usually establish several tricks.

Listed below are some of these combinations and how one might correctly finesse:

> = denotes the first card played.
>
> \- denotes the second card played IF opponent plays low.

A **simple finesse** is taken when only one key card is missing:

(1)	A<u>Q</u>	(2)	A98<u>7</u>	(3)	<u>Q</u>J10	(4)	AQ<u>J</u>
	9<u>8</u>		<u>Q</u>J10		A6<u>4</u>		65<u>4</u>

To **finesse the left-hand opponent** for a missing honor:

(1)	<u>K</u>9	(2)	<u>K</u>Q9	(3)	Q8<u>6</u>	(4)	KJ<u>10</u>
	7<u>6</u>		8<u>3</u>		<u>A</u>43		65<u>4</u>

On (1) immediately above, lead toward the King. On (2) and (4), as always when you need to finesse twice, go back to the closed hand in another suit. On (3) immediately above, play the Ace, then lead small toward the Queen. If left-hand opponent has the King, he will invariably play it for fear declarer has a doubleton. This play (3) is the only possibility to make two tricks out of this combination.

To **finesse the right-hand** opponent for a missing honor and/or if you are in the dummy for the last time, you may make a **backward finesse**.

(1)	<u>K</u>J10	Play to the King then play the Jack and insert the 8
	A8<u>7</u>	
(2)	<u>A</u>754	Play to the Ace then small toward the Jack
	KJ<u>10</u>	
(3)	J<u>92</u>	Play the 9 first, discard the 4, play the Jack, discard the 10, then play the 2 to the long hand (an unblocking play)
	AQ10<u>4</u>	

SUMMARY OF ODDS
How Suits May Divide

Cards missing	Division	Approximate Percentage
6	3-3	36
6	4-2	48
5	3-2	68
4	3-1	50
4	2-2	41
4	4-0	10
3	2-1	78
3	3-0	22
2	1-1	52
2	2-0	48

This table is from an ACBL publication.

Adages

- An even number of cards held by opponents will divide unevenly most of the time.

- An odd number will divide as evenly as possible most of the time.

- Eight ever – nine never! Finesse for a missing Queen with 8 cards in the suit. Play for the fall of the Queen with 9 cards.

- With 10 cards in one suit, play straight for the fall of the missing King.

- Play for the Queen to be over the Jack.

- Don't send a boy to do a man's work. (Trump high if you think next chair may also be trumping.)

SUMMARY
ARCH

A →Analyze the Lead

- Top card in a sequence
- Fourth card down from longest and strongest suit
- A singleton
- A trump
- Top of nothing

R →Review the Bidding

- Where are the outstanding HCP's located

C →Count, Count, Count

- Count your cards, your HCP's and length points
- Count opponents' length and strength during the bidding
- Count winners in a notrump contract
- Count losers in a suit contract
- Count the cards in every suit as they fall – most especially the trump suit

H →How

1. Make a hold-up play (page 167)
2. Watch the timing (page 168)
3. Put a loser on a loser (page 169)
4. Unblock (page 170)
5. Crossruff (page 171)
6. Avoid dangerous opponent (page 173)
7. End play opponent (page 174)
8. Finesse (page 175)
9. Create an entry (page 176)
10. Make a safety play (page 177)

MOST IMPORTANT OF ALL:

DEVELOP THE BEST SIDE SUIT EARLY FOR DISCARDS AS SHOWN ON MOST HANDS PRESENTED FOR STUDY.

Declarer North 3 NT
None Vulnerable

The Play of the Hand
The Hold-up Play

North (dealer)
S A Q 3
H K Q 3
D Q J 10 6
C K 9 2

West
S J 9 7 6
H J 9
D K 3 2
C J 6 5 4

East
S 10 8 5
H A 10 6 5 4
D 7 4
C Q 8 7

South
S K 4 2
H 8 7 2
D A 9 8 5
C A 10 3

The Bidding: North 1 NT – East pass – South 3 NT, West pass, pass, pass.

The Lead: The 5 of hearts

The Play: South should hold up winning the first heart hoping West's hand will be void of hearts if he gains the lead.

Tips: In planning NT play, count your winners.

Many players would automatically win the heart lead. Observe what happens if declarer wins the first heart trick. His other honor will be captured by East if West gets in and still has a heart to lead to his partner.

After North wins a heart, he must finesse East for the diamond King. He cannot allow East to gain the lead.

Declarer South 4 Spades
None Vulnerable

The Play of the Hand
The Timing is Important

<u>**North**</u>
S 10 9 7 2
H K Q 4
D A 9 6
C J 8 6

<u>**West**</u>
S 4
H A 9 8 5
D Q J 10 5
C 7 5 3 2

<u>**East**</u>
S A K
H J 10 7 3
D 8 3 2
C Q 10 9 4

<u>**South**</u> (dealer)
S Q J 8 6 5 3
H 6 2
D K 7 4
C A K

The Bidding: South 1 spade – West pass – North 2 spades – East pass – South 3 spades – West pass – North 4 spades -- East pass, pass, pass.

The Lead: The Queen of diamonds

The Play: Win the diamond lead with the King in the closed hand. Play a **small heart toward the King** in dummy to establish a heart on which to discard a losing diamond. Note if you play a trump at trick two or three East will win and return a diamond.

Tip: Timing refers to the order in which declarer or defender plays his tricks. The timing is very important on practically every hand. Do we need to ruff losers in dummy before drawing trumps? Do we need to discard losers on an established suit – or do we need to establish a suit?? Analyze, review and count.

Declarer North 4 Hearts
None Vulnerable

The Play of the Hand
A Loser on a Loser

North
S J 6 2
H J 7 6 5
D A J
C 9 8 7 2

West
S A K Q 4
H 9 8 4 3 2
D 9 8
C Q 6

East
S 10 9 8 5 3
H --
D 10 4 3 2
C K J 10 3

South (dealer)
S 7
H A K Q 10
D K Q 7 6 5
C A 5 4

The Bidding: South 1 diamond – West pass – North 1 heart – East pass – South 4 hearts – West pass, pass, pass.

The Lead: The 10 of spades

The Play: On every hand, a declarer must consider how the trumps might break; that is the one suit on which he must maintain control. On this hand, he should discard dummy's losing clubs instead of trumping the spades. He can later run the diamond suit until West trumps. This would reduce West's trumps to the same number held by declarer.

Tip: It is often very important to test the trump suit early (when holding top honors) even when there are other things you wish to do before relinquishing the lead.

Declarer South 3 NT
None Vulnerable

The Play of the Hand
Unblocking to Create an Entry

North (dealer)
S 9
H A J 9 6 5 4
D A K
C J 8 3 2

West
S J 8 7 5 2
H K Q 10 8
D 4 2
C A 9

East
S K 10 6 4
H 7 3
D 6 5 3
C K 10 6 4

South
S A Q 3
H 2
D Q J 10 9 8 7
C Q 7 5

The Bidding: North 1 heart – East pass – South 2 diamonds – West pass – North 2 hearts – South 3 NT – West pass, pass, pass.

The Lead: The 5 of spades

The Play: South counts his winners – 6 diamonds, 2 spades, and the Ace of hearts. Transportation is a problem. Practical solution – allow East to win the King of spades. When he returns a spade, win with the Queen, play the Ace and discard the AK of diamonds.

Tip: Count winners in a notrump contract. There is no ruffing power!

Declarer East 4 Spades
None Vulnerable

The Play of the Hand
The Crossruff

North (dealer)
S J
H 6 4 3 2
D K 6 5 4 3 2
C Q J

West
S Q 9 8 4
H A J 8 7 5
D --
C 10 9 8 7

East
S A K 7 6 5 2
H --
D J 10 9 8 7
C A K

South
S 10 3
H K Q 10 9
D A Q
C 6 5 4 3 2

The Bidding: North pass – East 1 spade – South pass – West 3 spades – North pass – East 4 spades – South pass, pass, pass.

The Lead: The King of hearts

The Play: The most important thing to remember in crossruffing is to **cash all outside winners before beginning the crossruff** to avoid opponents trumping winners later in the play. Win the Ace of hearts, discard a diamond. Cash the AK of clubs, ruff a diamond, ruff a heart, etc. etc. Ruff first tricks with small trumps while opponents must still follow suit.

Tip: On some hands, it is better to NEVER draw trumps. Declarer will take all trumps separately. The type of hand that plays better by crossruffing is a hand with plenty of trumps in both hands. Each hand might also contain a singleton or doubleton in different suits and/or a void in both hands in different suits.

Declarer South 3 NT
None Vulnerable

The Play of the Hand
When NOT to Make a Hold-up Play

North
S J 10 3
H 7 4
D A Q 9 5 4
C Q 8 6

West
S 9 5
H K Q J 10
D J 8 3 2
C K J 7

East
S 8 7 6 4 2
H 9 6 5 3
D 7
C A 10 9

South (dealer)
S A K Q
H A 8 2
D K 10 6
C 5 4 3 2

The Bidding: South 1 NT – West pass – North 3 NT – East pass, pass, pass.

The Lead: The King of hearts

The Play: It is of no use to hold up in a suit with so few cards as it would be difficult to deplete either of opponents' hand in the heart suit. Win the Ace of hearts, play a small diamond to the Ace and a small diamond back to closed hand, winning the King. Finesse West for the Jack and run your winners.

Tip: When holding the combination of cards in this diamond suit, try to play in a manner that will allow you to detect how the cards are divided.

Declarer South 5 Spades
None Vulnerable

The Play of the Hand
Establishing a Suit on which to Discard Losers
Watching Entries and Dangerous Opponent

North
S J 9 4
H A 2
D A J 10 9 8 7
C 6 5

West
S 5
H K Q J 10 7 3
D 6 2
C A 10 9 8

East
S 8 3
H 9 8 6 5
D K Q 4
C Q J 7 4

South (dealer)
S A K Q 10 7 6 2
H 4
D 5 3
C K 3 2

The Bidding: South 1 spade – West 2 hearts – North 3 diamonds – East 3 hearts – South 4 spades – West 5 hearts – North 5 spades – East pass, pass, pass.

The Lead: The King of hearts

The Play: Allow West to win the King of hearts, win the second heart and discard a diamond. Play the Ace of diamonds and trump a diamond HIGH – play the 6 of spades to the 9 and trump another diamond HIGH. Play the Jack of spades, overtake in closed hand and play the **carefully preserved** 2 of spades to the 4 and discard the losing clubs on the diamond suit.

Tip: East is the dangerous opponent. If he gains the lead, he will lead a club through South's unprotected King.

174

Declarer North 4 Spades
None Vulnerable

The Play of the Hand
Counting and Stripping
the Hand for an End Play

North (dealer)
S A Q J 10 9 2
H K Q 9 8
D K 10
C 2

West
S 5 4 3
H 5 4 3
D 9 3 2
C Q 5 4 3

East
S --
H J 6 2
D A Q J 5 4
C A J 9 8 7

South
S K 8 7 6
H A 10 7
D 8 7 6
C K 10 6

The Bidding: North 1 spade – East 2 diamonds – South 2 spades – West pass – North 3 hearts – East 4 clubs – South 4 spades – West pass, pass, pass.

The Lead: The 2 of hearts

Analyzing: Declarer assumes 10 of East's cards are in diamonds and clubs and that he has most of the outstanding honor count to make two bids. The small heart lead suggests a 3-card suit, so East may be void in the trump suit.

The Play: North wins the heart lead, draws the outstanding trumps and plays the hearts – discarding a small diamond from the dummy. Declarer now plays the 2 of clubs toward the King forcing East to win and lead into his hand.

Tip: Listen to the bidding carefully in order to place the outstanding high cards. The lead also "tells a story."

Declarer South 7 Clubs
None Vulnerable

The Play of the Hand
Finessing with Confidence

North
S A 9 8 4
H A K 8
D --
C A K J 4 3 2

West
S J 10 5
H J 10 7 5
D J 5 3 2
C 9 6

East
S 7 2
H 6 4
D K 10 9 8 7 6 4
C Q 5

South (dealer)
S K Q 6 3
H Q 9 3 2
D A Q
C 10 8 7

The Bidding: South 1 club – North 1 spade – East pass – South 2 spades – North 4 NT – South 5 diamonds – North 7 clubs – East pass, pass, pass.

The Lead: The Jack of hearts

The Play: North wins with the Ace of hearts, draws trumps, leads a small heart toward dummy and plays the 8 if West doesn't play high. He comes back to closed hand, discards a spade on the long heart and trumps remaining losers.

Tips: Declarer "analyzed the lead." The lead of the Jack promises the 10.

North got cold feet about a small slam in spades because of the quality of his suit and decided to go for a "grand" in clubs.

Declarer South 4 Spades
None Vulnerable

The Play of the Hand
Preserving Trumps to Create an Entry

North
S K Q 2
H 5 4 3
D 4 3
C A K 5 4 3

West
S 6 5
H Q J 10 9
D Q 9 7 6
C 9 6 2

East (dealer)
S 8 4
H K 6 2
D A J 10 8 2
C Q J 10

South
S A J 10 9 7 3
H A 8 7
D K 5
C 8 7

The Bidding: East pass – South 1 spade – West pass – North 2 clubs – East 2 diamonds – South 2 spades – West pass – North 4 spades -- East pass, pass, pass.

The Lead: The 6 of diamonds

The Play: South wins the second diamond, cashes the Ace of spades, cashes AK of clubs, trumps a club with a high spade – goes to dummy with a trump and discards 2 losing hearts on the clubs.

Tip: Little cards take tricks!

South played only 1 spade in case the clubs break 4/2 – which would require two entries in dummy to establish them.

Declarer South 3 NT
None Vulnerable

The Play of the Hand
Avoiding the Dangerous Opponent
The Safety Play

<table>
<tr><td></td><td>North
S 8 5
H A 8 7 4
D A 10 8 5 3
C 8 2</td><td></td></tr>
<tr><td>West
S Q 10 7 6 3
H Q J 9
D 7
C 10 9 5 4</td><td></td><td>East
S K J 4
H 10 6 5 3
D Q J 9 6 4
C Q</td></tr>
<tr><td></td><td>South (dealer)
S A 9 2
H K 2
D K 2
C A K J 7 6 3</td><td></td></tr>
</table>

The Bidding: South 1 club – West pass – North 1 diamond – South 3 NT – West pass, pass, pass.

The Lead: The 6 of spades

The Play: Win the third spade, go to the board and play a club. Let East hold the trick. Win any suit he returns and cash your winners.

Tip: To avoid the dangerous opponent declarer must plan the play BEFORE he begins running off winners.

If East's Queen is a singleton, as suspected since second hand usually plays low, then West's 10 of clubs would develop as a winner. To guard against West gaining the lead and cashing his spade winners, declarer gives up a trick to East.

There are numerous situations where a safety play is needed; therefore, it is important to consider the theory behind them as opposed to trying to memorize each situation in which one may be needed.

CHAPTER TEN: THE DEFENSE OF THE HAND

The defense of a contract is a race with declarer. He is considering where his offensive tricks are coming from; you are considering where the defensive tricks are coming from.

To state this simply, both declarer and defender need to determine goals and make a **plan early in the play**. Defenders need to understand when to make hold-up plays and safety plays; how to maintain communication between the two hands; when to return partner's suit and when to switch and "to which to switch."

A partnership understanding should be reached on discarding. For instance, defenders need a plan for one to protect one suit when discarding (declarer is running a long, established suit) while the other protects a different suit. A spot card 6 or above, may be used to tell partner you are protecting that suit. If you cannot afford to discard from the suit you are protecting, play a very low card from a suit in which you have **no interest and follow with a higher card**.

A partnership must learn to read each other's signals. Every card tells a story. Understanding the defensive signals discussed in this chapter makes defending a hand just as much fun as playing a hand.

The defense also needs to keep count on **every suit** in order to make little cards count.

The Role of
The Opening Leader

The opening lead in suit or notrump play often sets the stage for the defense. The correct opening lead can sometimes defeat the opponents in the first few plays. Some of the standard leads are listed below **by priority**.

- Lead partner's suit
- Lead your suit
- Lead the top of a sequence
- Lead the top of an interior sequence in notrump
- Lead the fourth from the longest and strongest suit
- Lead a singleton in a suit bid
- Lead the top of nothing

A Standard Lead Table at the end of this chapter will show the exact card to lead from the suit you choose to lead.

The Role of Second Hand

In general, second hand plays low in a suit or notrump contract, since his partner still has an opportunity to play. He plays high only when by doing so he might establish a winner for his partnership. When holding Kx and the QJ10 is in dummy, second hand would obviously cover declarer's lead. **As in all other rules and guidelines, common sense prevails.**

The Role of Third Hand

Third hand plays a very important role in defense. Third hand can usually tell by the opening lead whether partner has gotten off to an effective lead for his partnership. He can tell this by observing the card partner led, The Rule of

Eleven, by observing dummy, by observing his own holding in the suit led and by reviewing the bidding. If the opening leader's card holds, responder plays a 6 or higher to encourage partner or below a 6 to discourage.

If the opening lead is a 6 or under suggesting an honor in the suit led, third hand usually plays high – **but not always**. If the third hand wins the opening lead, he **usually** returns his partner's suit, **but not always**. If third hand thinks partner's suit holds the most promise for defeating the contract, he returns the suit immediately while partner has a possible entry:

- Holding touching honors, **he wins with the lowest** card and returns the highest.
- Holding Axx he wins with the Ace and returns the highest remaining card.
- If partner leads the King and third hand holds only two cards including the Ace, he overtakes the King and returns the small card to unblock.

If third hand doesn't win the first trick, but later gains the lead, he returns as follows:

- Holding 3 small cards, he returns the highest of the 2 remaining cards.
- Holding 4 small cards, he returns the lowest remaining card.
- When holding an honor and 2 small cards, he returns the honor in order to surround a high card held by opponent.

If third hand holds a very good suit that looks even more promising than partner's, he may assert his prerogative and return his own suit.

When to Make a Hold-up Play

Third hand must pay very close attention to dummy's holding. For instance, if dummy has Kxx – partner leads small showing he also holds an honor and third hand holds the Ace – he should usually keep that Ace to capture the King (discard a 6 or above to indicate interest.) If dummy holds KQx, third hand should usually let the first honor hold and cover the second honor. Again, signal high, if possible, to encourage partner. The object being to break communication between declarer and dummy. The general rule is **when dummy holds 1 honor and third hand holds a higher honor and a card as high as 9, he inserts the 9 and stays over dummy's one honor.** Third hand plays high if dummy has no honor card.

What to Discard

When declarer is playing a suit, defenders need a system for discarding. Some players use the first discard – 6 or above – to show interest and reiterate by discarding a lower card. In some instances they need to hold on to the suit they like and **discard very low from a suit they do not like. A high-low discard says "I like". A low-high discard says "I do not like."**

Third hand should try to keep parity with any suit in dummy.

PARTNERSHIP COMMUNICATION THROUGH DEFENSIVE SIGNALS

Card signals are an integral part of defensive bridge. Every card played has a message. The basic defensive signals are the **Attitude Signal**, the **Suit Preference Signal**, the **Count Signal** and the **Trump Count Signal**.

The Attitude Signal

The **Attitude Signal** tells partner whether or not you like his lead. It is used primarily **on partner's opening lead** but may be used in a subsequent play on any lead. The attitude signal may be used on weak or strong hands. A high card (6 or above) followed to partner's lead says, "I like it, I like it." A low card (5 or below) followed to partner's lead says "I have no interest in that suit." It possibly suggests a switch. It DOES NOT say which suit you do like, the discard can send only one message. (EXCEPTION) If there is a singleton in dummy, third hand shows suit preference. **If you play high, play the highest card you can afford**. For example, if you hold 10 9 8 7, play the 10. If you hold Q 9 8 7, play the 9.

Summary Attitude
High, I like it
Low, I don't like it

The Suit Preference Signal

The **Suit Preference Signal** is most commonly used **when returning a suit for partner to ruff**. He will thereby know in which suit you hold an additional entry so you can "sock it to the declarer" once again. When using the suit preference signal (or other signals) **do not consider the trump suit** or the suit being played at the moment. So that leaves only 2 suits to be considered. Return the highest card you can afford if your entry (preference) is in the higher-ranked suit. Return your lowest card if you want the lower-ranked suit returned. For example, your partner leads a singleton spade which you win with the Ace. (Hearts are trumps.) In addition to holding the Ace of spades, you also hold the Ace of clubs. So when you return a spade, the suit being played at the moment, return the lowest card you hold. Partner can safely return a club – you can give him another ruff. Poor opponents!

Summary Suit Preference
High card for higher-ranked suit Low card for lower- ranked suit

The Trump Echo

The **Trump Echo** is used to show the number of trumps held. **The play of a high (but not your highest) trump card followed by a low trump card shows 3 trumps. A low trump card followed by a higher trump card shows a holding of 2 or 4 trumps.** It is especially nice to know this when you can get a crossruff going during defense. (You are trumping one of declarer's suits – your partner is ruffing another.) **Note this is the exact opposite of giving count in other suits.** This allows you to hold on to your highest trump card.

Summary Trump Count
High-Low shows 3 trumps Low-High shows 2 trumps

The Count Signal

The **Count Signal** is usually applied **when following to declarer's lead**. A high-low **shows an even number of cards** in that suit. A **low-high shows an odd number of cards**. This is an especially helpful aid when opponents have one long semi-solid suit in dummy – no outside entry – and partner holds the top card. Your count tells partner how long to hold on to that top card so that declarer will be out of that suit and can no longer reach dummy.

Summary Count Signal

High-low shows an even number of cards
Low-high shows odd number of cards

Unfortunately, giving count is too often considered inconsequential in defense. However, it is of utmost importance for partner to know how many cards remain in a suit in which he is interested. Since his motives aren't always clear – **give count on all suits which you cannot cover in dummy**.

THE RULE OF ELEVEN

The Rule of Eleven is an invaluable aid in defense. It has been used in serious bridge games a very long time; yet it is seemingly overlooked by many players who may think it difficult. It is actually very simple.

The Rule of Eleven isn't a bridge rule; it is an aid that was supposedly discovered by a mathematician who happened to be a bridge player. The reason it works isn't widely known, if known at all, but it definitely works when partner has led the 4th card down from a suit (K 9 6 5 4).

The Rule of Eleven allows third hand to determine exactly how many cards declarer holds higher than the spot card led by his partner. He may do this by subtracting the spot (the value) on the card led from 11. See illustration below on a 3NT contract.

North (dummy)
H 5 3 2

West (second hand)   **East (third hand)**
H K 9 8 7̲   H Q J 6

South (declarer)
H A 10 4

West leads the 7 of hearts. Third hand subtracts 7 from 11, ascertaining that there are 4 cards held by himself, dummy and declarer higher than the 7. He sees dummy has none, so this leaves declarer with 2 cards higher than the 7.

The Rule enables third hand to decide whether his partner has made a helpful lead for the partnership. If not, third hand may switch to another suit when he gains the lead rather than routinely returning partner's suit. The Rule can be used on any contract as long as the lead is fourth card down in the suit. It is particularly helpful in notrump contracts.

SUMMARY AND TIPS ON COMMUNICATION

- Do not high-low with Qx; when you throw the Queen you promise the Jack or a singleton. Partner is expected to switch to a lower card when he sees your Queen.

- The discard of an unusually high card when it is obvious it is not suit preference asks for a shift to the higher ranking suit.

- When you are leading a suit and partner plays a low card, its primary purpose is to show no strength. Don't "eat" your high cards. If dummy has a long side suit, it is **usually** best to take your winners.

- Both members of a partnership must be aware that the other may not always hold a high card (6 or above) that can be safely expended. Therefore, if a 4 is the highest card you can afford to discard to show your attitude, follow even lower with the next card – a high-low is also encouraging. If you want to discourage, play the 3 and then the 4; a low-high is discouraging.

- When you have led a suit because of the safety of playing it – in other words not the suit in which you have the AQ or KJ and partner is later on lead, throw the smallest card from the suit you originally led to discourage partner from returning your lead.

- If partner leads the King of a suit, and you hold the Ax, overtake with the Ace and return the low card to unblock.

- Do not play high-low on partner's lead if you don't need the suit continued – for instance if you can't over-ruff dummy, don't ask partner to continue the suit.

- When dummy holds a singleton in the suit your partner leads, you should show suit preference, not attitude.

- Do not signal with a card that might eventually take a trick.

- Try to keep parity with dummy's holding. If he holds 4 cards you should try to keep 4 of the same suit.

- When declarer is running a long suit, try to discard from the suit(s) he knows you hold. If declarer has a "good suit" in dummy and you must discard while he is running another suit, try to keep cards in "dummy's" good suit to protect partner and "obscure" opponent.

- When giving count on an evenly divided suit, discard the highest card you can afford. With an odd number of cards, begin with your lowest one (6 5 4 3 <u>2</u>).

LEADS
Opening Leads Against Suit Bids

Like many other aspects of playing bridge, **to select the best opening lead requires concentration and counting** during the bidding process, an understanding of why and when some leads are more effective than others AND a firm resolve to find a way to defeat the opponents on every hand if at all possible. What makes bridge so interesting is the competition it evokes. Informed leads help get the defense off to a good competitive start.

Before considering the various recommendations on making an effective opening lead, let's consider a few "be awares" and "avoids."

- Avoid leading a suit bid by an opponent, especially those that contain 5 cards. A lead through dummy's unsupported 4-card suit is often profitable.

- Avoid leading a suit partner could have bid on the one level. He probably lacked sufficient cards.

- Be aware of partner's failure to make a lead-directing double of artificial bids, (Stayman, Gerber, transfers, etc.).

- Avoid leading a worthless doubleton unless partner has bid the suit.

- Avoid depending upon partner when all HCP's are accounted for by the opponents' bidding and your hand. For instance, how many HCP's can partner have with the following bidding:

Opponent	You	Opponent	Partner
1 NT (16)	12 HCP's	3 NT (10)	2 HCP's

Don't expect to hit partner; you're on your own!

When Partner has Bid

If you love your partner and want him to be happy, **LEAD HIS SUIT** unless you have a really good reason not to, such as:

- You have a side-suit singleton and the Ace of trumps.

- You have a very good suit headed by AK AND an early trump entry.

- You forgot what he bid! (You couldn't!)

When undecided whether to lead your suit or partner's in a highly competitive situation, you may wish to lead whichever suit that contains an Ace to see the board and "hear" from partner. Above all, if you lead partner's suit, LEAD THE CORRECT CARD. If you hold his Ace and you lead his suit, lead the Ace. If you hold touching honors, lead the top card. Always lead the top card when holding only 2 cards in a suit. (See Lead Table).

Was Opponents' Bidding Active or Passive

If opponents have been **PASSIVE** (you hear a few sighs or groans along the way and they seem as though they don't know where or how high to land), a **PASSIVE LEAD** is called for:

Opponent	You	Opponent	Partner
1 heart	pass	1 spade	pass
1 notrump	pass	2 clubs	pass
2 spades	pass	pass	pass

It sounds as though opponents have a misfit. This is the time to make a passive lead that will not help opponents NOR hurt your partner. The best lead in a suit contract is from a sequence of touching honors KQJ, AK5, QJ95 etc. With no sequence, lead a small card from three or four cards with an honor. If (in the previously mentioned hand) you can't lead from the unbid diamond suit, a club lead is another possibility ... leading <u>through</u> <u>strength</u> up to weakness. Do not lead into declarer's suit unless you have a strong sequence lead even if he has shown only 4 cards.

If the opponents are bidding **TWO SUITS STRONGLY** ... (each showing support for the other) **ACTIVE DEFENSE** is called for. One suit will be trumps and the other will be used for discards. Lead one of the unbid suits even if you must make a usual "no-no" lead. Lead an Ace without the King, lead from an AQ or KJ combination, etc. If really desperate to defeat the opponents, you might even try the King from Kx in <u>an</u> <u>unbid</u> <u>suit</u> in hopes of getting a ruff. (Note: if you try this lead and it backfires, tell your bridge friends you forgot just where the idea was suggested.) If opponents have bid a side suit strongly and you have several cards in that suit, consider the possibility that partner may be void in the suit. Do something audacious when opponents have strongly bid two suits!

When to Lead Trumps

If opponents have bid two suits ... landing in the second ... and **YOU HAVE DECLARER'S FIRST-BID SUIT, LEAD A TRUMP.**

Opponent	You	Opponent	Partner
1 spade	pass	2 hearts	pass
4 hearts	pass	pass	pass

If you hold K Q 10 9 in spades (previous hand), opponent will hold 3 or 4 little cards that he hopes to ruff in dummy. The lead of a trump will decrease his ability to do so.

Another time a **TRUMP LEAD** is productive … in fact, it is "demanded" by most bridge experts, is <u>when</u> <u>your</u> <u>partner</u> <u>has</u> <u>left</u> <u>in</u> <u>your</u> <u>low-level</u> **TAKEOUT DOUBLE**:

Opponent	You	Opponent	Partner
1 heart	double	pass	pass

The hands:

North Opponent
S K Q
H Q 10 9 8 7
D Q 5
C K Q 7 6

Partner (West)	**You (East)**
S 8 7 5	S A J 10 9
H A K 6 5 4 2	H 3
D K 10 9	D A J 8 7
C 8	C A J 10 9

South Opponent
Immaterial

You (East) should lead your heart and allow partner to decide whether to continue a trump lead. Most experts would lead another trump (West) but; it is lots of fun and sometimes more productive to lead through strength and get in a few "low-level" ruffs.

Finally a **TRUMP LEAD** is called for **when opponents are trying to crossruff a hand**. The bidding might go as follows:

Opponent	You	Opponent	Partner
1 heart	pass	4 hearts	pass

As we know, the above bid by responder usually shows a weak hand with 5 hearts, an outside Ace and a singleton. We also know if there is a singleton in one hand, the other three players may also have a singleton and unusual distribution.

The above bidding (1 heart – 4 hearts) is a clue that opponents may crossruff the hand; or, it may not be known until the play progresses whether declarer will crossruff. In either case, the defense should lead a trump as soon as it is known a crossruff is on the horizon. Lead a trump when opponents sacrifice, to cut down on crossruffing.

Subsequent Leads

When you have led partner's suit and partner wins dummy's card with a low card (declarer cannot cover), partner should try to hit you in another suit so you can lead through dummy again. Third hand must not return the suit if the high cards are visible. He should "stay over dummy". If you don't get in again, declarer must eventually break the suit.

	Dummy S K 10 8 7	
You S 5 3 2		**Partner** S A Q 9 6
	Declarer S J 4	

When you do return the same suit partner led, RETURN THE CORRECT CARD as discussed under The Defense of the Hand. Every card tells a story … make sure you and partner are telling the same one!

Opening Leads Against Notrump Contracts

Good notrump leads are often more easily defined than leads against a suit contract – especially when the bidding has gone 1 NT – 3 NT. Rarely will there be more than two choices.

1. **A SEQUENCE LEAD**:
   (a) The top card from a solid sequence, (A K Q J).
   (b) The top card from a broken sequence, (Q J 9 7).
   (c) The top card from an interior sequence, (K J 10 9).
2. **THE 4TH CARD DOWN** from the longest, strongest suit, (K J 9 8 4).
3. With none of the above, lead the "top of nothing" – 9 7 6 so partner will know you have no honor card.

Leads against notrump contracts preceded by suit bids require more concentration. Ask yourself after each bid or pass – what did I learn!

Opponent 1	You	Opponent 2	Partner
1 club	pass	1 heart	pass
2 notrump	pass	3 notrump	pass

What we know about opponent 1:

- He has 18-19 points.
- He doesn't have 4 hearts or 4 spades.
- He probably has a long club suit with stoppers in diamonds and spades.

What we know about opponent 2:

- He has at least 4 hearts and could have 4 spades.
- He has 7+ points.
- He has no more than 5 hearts and probably balanced distribution with at least 1 or 2 clubs.

The lead? A sequence from diamonds or spades. The second choice,

4th best. Try to see dummy before attacking the heart suit unless you have a very

good holding in hearts.

Now consider the best lead if the bidding goes as follows:

Opponent	You	Opponent	Partner
1 spade	pass	2 hearts	pass
3 clubs	pass	3 diamonds	pass
3 notrump	pass	pass	pass

- Avoid a spade or heart lead. Each opponent has 5 cards in the majors.
- Opponent 2 may have only 4 diamonds. Opponent 1 may have only 3 or 4 clubs. (Each opponent is "fishing" for a notrump contract.)
- With equal holdings in diamonds and clubs, lead diamonds. A club lead would be right into the "teeth" of declarer's hand. If he holds K J 9 8, the lead would finesse partner and help the opponent.

Some experts recommend leading an Ace against a small slam.

However, if you hold a KQ in one suit and the Ace of another suit, consider

leading the King and try for 2 tricks. Cashing two tricks against a small slam is

lots of fun!

When partner doubles ANY **uncontested notrump contract**, he is calling

for the **lead of the first-bid suit of dummy**.

When partner doubles a slam in a suit bid, he is calling for an

unusual lead. If either you or partner have bid, DO NOT lead your suit nor his.

Do not lead a trump. He usually has a void and wishes to ruff that suit. Consider opponents' side suit especially if you have length in that suit. This convention is called the **Lightner Slam Double**.

Subsequent Leads

The one lead most devastating to the defense is when third hand routinely "returns partner's lead." It seems the one misnomer always remembered is "return partner's suit." The opener often makes a blind lead. Subsequent leads are not blind leads. You will have seen dummy, heard from partner; and will have used the Rule of Eleven. Listed below are three hands that require logic as opposed to loyalty to a slogan.

Example 1

Opponent (dummy)
S K J 9 3
H 9 8
D 10 8 7 6
C A K 2

West (partner)
S Q 10 6 4
H A 5 4 3
D 9 5 4 3
C 8

East (you)
S A 7 2
H Q J 10 2
D 2
C 9 6 5 4 3

Opponent (declarer)
S 8 5
H K 7 6
D A K Q J
C Q J 10 7

The contract is 3 NT. Partner leads the 4 of spades, the fourth card down from his longest and strongest suit. Using the Rule of Eleven ...11-4 leaves 7 cards out higher than the 4 in dummy, your hand and declarer's hand. Since you can see 5 of those cards, you know declarer has 2. BUT, as you can also see, declarer's hand is not the hand containing strength in the spade suit.

Therefore, East will finesse his partner and help declarer if he wins and returns a spade. He wants to lead through the strength of declarer, up to weakness (dummy). He should switch to the Queen of hearts. Hearts is the best source for additional tricks … especially if West holds the Ace. In that case, declarer's King is trapped.

Example 2

North (dummy)
S J 5
H Q J 7
D 10 9
C A K Q 8 7 6

West (partner)
S Q 8 6 2
H 6 5 4
D A Q 7 6
C 3 2

East (you)
S A 4 3
H K 9 3 2
D 5 4 3 2
C 10 9

South (dealer and declarer)
S K 10 9 7
H A 10 8
D K J 8
C J 5 4

The contract is 3 NT, South. West's opening lead is the 2 of spades. East should win the Ace of spades; he should not return a spade. If West's honor in spades is the King, he can take it … if and when he gets in with another suit. Any time you see a long, strong suit in dummy and you know declarer has at least 3 cards in that suit, wake up. (South opens one club.) Declarer will win, run his 6 club tricks and finesse to win East's King of hearts. The lead of the 2 tells East his partner has only 4 cards in the spade suit. The only hope to defeat declarer is to switch to the diamond suit, leading through strength (South) up to weakness (North).

Example 3

North (dummy)
S J
H K J 9 5
D 10 8 7 6
C J 9 6 2

West (partner)
S 8 5 3 2
H 6 3
D A 5 3 2
C Q 7 4

East (you)
S A 6 4
H A Q 10 8 7
D Q J 9
C 5 3

South (declarer)
S K Q 10 9 7
H 4 2
D K 4
C A K 10 8

The contract is 3 clubs in the South. West leads the 6 of hearts, the suit partner overcalled. East wins North's 9 with the 10. He should not lead another heart immediately and establish a winner for the opposition. East needs to shift to the Queen of diamonds, hoping West can win and lead another heart. If West holds a singleton heart, declarer will have to lead hearts to East or East can cash out when he gets in with diamonds or spades. Most of the time, Aces will not go away. If partner has led a top card from a sequence, the story is different. A 4th best lead may contain a single top card as opposed to a 3-card sequence.

STANDARD LEAD TABLE
Leads Listed in Order of Preference

LEADS AGAINST SUIT CONTRACTS

* **If partner bid, lead his suit**

  Low with three or four cards: Q 6 <u>4</u>   K 8 4 <u>2</u>   9 6 <u>2</u>
  High from a doubleton: <u>6</u> 5   <u>K</u> 2   <u>Q</u> 7   <u>10</u> 7
  Top of a sequence: <u>K</u> Q J x   <u>K</u> Q 8 6   <u>Q</u> J 10 x
  Top of a broken sequence: <u>Q</u> J 9 x   <u>J</u> 10 8 x
  With AKx: Lead the Ace
  With AK doubleton: Lead the King
* (Some players prefer leading high **if** they **have supported the suit**.)

LEADS AGAINST NOTRUMP

Top of a sequence: <u>K</u> Q J x   <u>Q</u> J 10 x   <u>J</u> 10 9 x
Top of an interior sequence: A <u>Q</u> J 10   K <u>J</u> 10 9
Top of a broken sequence: <u>Q</u> J 9 x   <u>J</u> 10 8 x
Fourth down from longest and strongest: A J x <u>x</u>   K x x <u>x</u> x x

If partner bid, lead his suit

Low from 3 or 4: Q 8 <u>6</u>   Q 8 6 <u>5</u>
High from 2: <u>K</u> 2   <u>Q</u> 7   <u>6</u> 5
Top card from a sequence: <u>K</u> Q J   <u>Q</u> J 10   <u>J</u> 10 9

LEADS AGAINST DOUBLED NOTRUMP CONTRACTS

When partner doubles a notrump contract

- Lead his suit
- Lead your suit
- If both of you have bid a suit, lead yours
- If neither of you has bid a suit, lead dummy's first-bid suit
- Lead from weakest major suit. Partner has a long suit
  and an outside entry

The double of <u>all</u> artificial bids is lead directing (cue bids, Gerber, etc.)
The double of a slam in a suit contract calls for an unusual lead **not** the suit your partnership has bid **nor** a trump. (See Lightner Slam Double page 75..)

LEADS

SUMMARY AND TIPS

- If partner bid, lead his suit.

- If partner made a takeout double, the suits inferred by the double may hold promise.

- Lead a singleton.

- If opponents have bid aggressively, make an aggressive lead; if they bid passively, make a passive lead.

- If you have a strong suit and a nice holding in the trump suit, keep leading your suit to reduce opponents' trump holding. But do not give a ruff-sluff.

- If opponents bid a suit in which you have a good holding but they landed in another suit, lead a trump.

- If the bidding indicates opponents may crossruff, lead a trump.

- If partner left in your takeout double, lead a trump.

- With similar holdings in a major and minor, tend to lead the major. A good major suit holding is rarely suppressed in the bidding … the minors are.

- A strong 4-card sequence lead (K Q 10 9), even a 3-card sequence (K Q J) is preferred over a weak, longer suit (J 8 5 4 3). A partnership would need to "get in" several times to establish and reach such a suit.

- If Stayman is used, the "user" has at least 4 cards in one major. With a 2-diamond response from NT opener, his hand contains more cards in the minors.

- When absolutely broke and your lead must be from a weak suit with no honor card, lead the top card (8 6 5) so partner will not expect an honor from your hand.

- In order for a holding to be considered a broken sequence, only one number is omitted in the grouping. It is always the third card (Q J 9 4, the 10 is missing – K Q 10, the Jack is missing). Lead the top card.

- The use of the Rule of Eleven is absolutely essential to good defense of any contract when the fourth best is led.

- Review the Lead Table often to learn which card to lead from the suit you choose.

- Note that there may be a difference in leads when partner has bid and/or doubled. It is noted on Lead Table.

- Double any artificial bid if you want that suit led. If you do not double the artificial bid, partner will dismiss its potential.

- If partner has bid a suit, leading his suit takes precedence over other suggestions. However, if you hold an outside AK combination, you may choose to lead your Ace and "see" partner's attitude.

- **Against a small slam** suit contract, make an aggressive lead (Ax, KQx, QJ9, – even Kx as last resort.)

- **Against a small notrump slam**, make a passive lead. **Do not lead from an unsupported honor** (Kxx, Qxx, Jxx). The declarer is probably looking for that particular honor.

- **Against a grand slam**, make a safe, passive lead. A trump lead is usually safe unless you hold an honor.

- Against a doubled suit slam, look for an unusual lead: not your suit, not a trump, not partner's suit, **not necessarily** the first bid suit of dummy. Partner (doubler) may have a void – for instance, if opponents have strongly bid an outside suit and you hold cards in that suit.

Declarer South 6 spades
None Vulnerable

The Defense of the Hand
Judging Suit Preference by Counting
and Analyzing

North (dealer)
S K Q 2
H A J 8
D 10 5
C Q J 9 8 3

West
S 6
H 9 5 4
D 9 8 4 3
C A K 7 6 2

East
S 8 5 3
H 10 7 6 3 2
D Q J 7 6
C 4

South
S A J 10 9 7 4
H K Q
D A K 2
C 10 5

The Bidding: North 1 club – East pass – South 1 spade – West pass – North 2 spades – East pass – South 4 NT – West pass – North 5 diamonds – East pass – South 6 spades – West pass, pass, pass.

The Lead: The Ace of clubs

The Defense: West considers his partner's play of the 4. If his partner held two clubs, he would discard his highest card – which would have to be the 5 or 10 (West could see all other spots). Therefore, the 4 was the only club held by East. West continues with the King to defeat the contract.

Tips: The suggestion that one shouldn't ask for the number of Aces and Kings held by partner when he holds 2 losers in any <u>unbid</u> suit might be extended to "don't assume partner has the Ace in the suit he opened."

Since South needed to know North's specific Ace, he should have begun a cue bid sequence after the trump suit was established.

Declarer South 6 notrump
None Vulnerable

The Defense of the Hand
Communicating with Discards

North
S K 7 6
H K 4
D K Q J 10 6
C 7 3 2

West
S J 10 9 4
H 10 9 3 2
D 8 7 5
C K 4

East
S 5 3 2
H J 7 6
D 3 2
C Q J 10 9 8

South (dealer)
S A Q 8
H A Q 8 5
D A 9 4
C A 6 5

The Bidding: South 2NT – West pass – North 4 clubs – East pass – South 4 diamonds (shows 0 or 4 aces) – West pass – North 5 clubs – East pass – South 5 diamonds – West pass – North 6 NT – East pass, pass, pass.

When asking for Aces, use Gerber after notrump bids – including after a quantitative notrump response to a suit bid (1 club – 2NT – "4 clubs".)

The Lead: The Jack of spades

The Defense: South wins the spade lead and runs diamonds. East's first discard should be the Queen of clubs. This tells partner he has the Q J 10 (minimum) and that clubs is the suit he is protecting. West will discard according to what South is discarding.

Tip: Try to **discard** from the suit **declarer knows** you hold.

Declarer South 3 NT
None Vulnerable

The Defense of the Hand
When Defending Notrump Contracts

North
S K 5
H 8 3
D 6 3
C K Q J 10 9 8 7

West (dealer)
S Q J 9 6 4
H A K J 9 4
D 10 8
C 2

East
S 3 2
H 6 5 2
D A Q 9 7 2
C 6 5 4

South
S A 10 8 7
H Q 10 7
D K J 5 4
C A 3

The Bidding: West 1 spade – North 3 clubs – East pass – South 3 NT – West pass, pass, pass.

The Lead: The Ace of hearts

The Defense: East plays the 2 of hearts, giving count and denying an honor. West, seeing the long club suit reasons: the only hope to defeat the contract is to "hit" partner with the Ace of diamonds – BINGO. East wins, returns a heart trapping South's honor and thus defeats the contract. With two suits, lead the one with the AK, it surprises declarer and delights partner.

Tip: When partner leads an Ace defending a notrump contract – discard any honor card to unblock and to let partner in on "the know".

Declarer South 3 NT
None Vulnerable

The Defense of the Hand
Retaining Communication with Partner

North (dealer)
S K J 3 2
H A Q 5
D 7
C Q J 10 9 4

West
S 9 8 6 5
H 9 8 4 3 2
D 8 2
C K 5

East
S 7 4
H J 7
D A K J 10 6 5 4
C 8 2

South
S A Q 10
H K 10 6
D Q 9 3
C A 7 6 3

The Bidding: North 1 club – East 2 diamonds – South 3 NT – West pass, pass, pass.

The Lead: The 8 of diamonds

The Defense: Since East has no outside entry, his best hope for defeating the contract is to insert the 10 and allow South to take a trick in diamonds. This allows East and West to retain communication. Hopefully West has one more diamond and will have an opportunity to gain the lead. If this is not the case, the contract is unbeatable.

Tip: It is important to "include partner" in arriving at a decision. Treat both hands as a whole.

Declarer South 3 NT
None Vulnerable

The Defense of the Hand
Giving Count when Defending Notrump Contracts

North
S 10 4 3
H A Q 5
D 7 5
C K Q J 10 4

West
S 6 5
H 7 3 2
D A K J 6 3 2
C 7 3

East (dealer)
S A 9 8 7 2
H 9 8 4
D 9 4
C 6 5 2

South
S K Q J
H K J 10 6
D Q 10 8
C A 9 8

The Bidding: East pass – South 1 NT – West pass – North 3 NT – East pass, pass, pass.

The Lead: The Ace of diamonds

The Defense: Count is given by third hand when defending against notrump contracts when partner leads an Ace or when third hand has no card higher than dummy's.

Tips: Third hand should drop an honor card (K Q J) if he holds one. Therefore, when East plays the 9, he is denying holding an honor.

Since West has no outside entry to his hand, he must switch to another suit in hopes of hitting partner. West has the Ace of diamonds, dummy has the Ace of hearts. West tries the spade 6 while there is a chance for East to still hold a diamond (as opposed to laying down the King.)

Giving count – High/low shows an <u>even</u> number of cards.
Low/high shows an <u>odd</u> number of cards.

Declarer South 6 Spades
None Vulnerable

The Defense of the Hand
When to Cover

North
S J 4
H A Q
D A 8 7 6 5
C A K 8 6

West
S K 3
H J 9 8 2
D Q 10 9
C Q J 10 4

East
S Q 5
H 10 7 6 5 3
D 4 2
C 9 7 3 2

South (dealer)
S A 10 9 8 7 6 2
H K 4
D K J 3
C 5

The Bidding: South 1 spade – West pass – North 2 diamonds – East pass – South 3 diamonds – West pass – North 4 clubs – East pass – South 4 spades – West pass – North 5 spades – East pass – South 6 spades – West pass, pass, pass.

The Lead: The Queen of clubs

The Defense: Declarer wins the club and plays the Jack of spades. East has listened to the bidding and deduces the spade suit is weak. He covers the Jack in hopes of setting up a winner for partner.

Tip: Second hand plays high only when he thinks he will set up a trick for partner, wants declarer to be in a certain hand, or if the honor will win the trick.

Declarer South 3 NT
None Vulnerable

The Defense of the Hand
Notrump Defense
Giving Count

North
S Q 10 9
H K 2
D J 10 9 4
C A 8 7 6

West
S A J 7 6 5
H J 10 3
D K 5
C 9 3 2

East
S 8 3 2
H Q 9 8 7 6
D 8 3 2
C K 5

South (dealer)
S K 4
H A 5 4
D A Q 7 6
C Q J 10 4

The Bidding: South 1 NT – West pass – North 3 NT – East pass, pass, pass.

The Lead: The 6 of spades

The Defense: Since East cannot cover the 10 played from dummy, he gives count. To show an **odd** number of cards, he plays the lowest card – the 2. This enables West to count the cards remaining in declarer's hand.

Tip: Every card tells a story. Be a helpmate to partner even when you hold uneventful cards.

Declarer South 3 NT
None Vulnerable

The Defense of the Hand
Notrump Defense
Negative Discards

North
S J 10 3 2
H Q 6 5
D K J 8
C K J 10

West
S A 9 8 5 4
H 8 4
D 7 6 5
C 8 5 4

East
S --
H A K J 10
D 10 9 4 3 2
C 7 6 3 2

South (dealer)
S K Q 7 6
H 9 7 3 2
D A Q
C A Q 9

The Bidding: South 1 NT – West pass – North 3 NT – East pass, pass, pass.

The Lead: The 5 of spades

The Defense: East discards the 2 of diamonds, **I Don't Like Diamonds!** East's next discard is the 2 of clubs, **I Don't Like Clubs Either!** West must "hop up" with his Ace of spades ASAP and play the 8 of hearts.

Tip: Now, assume – that late in the play – for illustration only – your partner had already taken the defensive book and your earlier discards were two sevens because they were the lowest cards you held – discard the Jack of hearts – if your partner is sleepy, discard the Ace!

Declarer South 3 NT
None Vulnerable

The Defense of the Hand
Stayman
The Rule of Eleven

North
S 9 8
H J 10 9 2
D A K J 2
C Q 6 5

West (dealer)
S A J 7 6 3
H 8 5 4
D 8 7 5
C 7 4

East
S Q 10 5
H A 7 6
D 4 3
C J 10 9 3 2

South
S K 4 2
H K Q 3
D Q 10 9 6
C A K 8

The Bidding: West pass – North pass – East pass – South 1 NT – West pass – North 2 clubs – East pass – South 2 diamonds – West pass – North 3 NT – East pass, pass, pass.

The Lead: The 6 of spades

The Defense: East uses the Rule of Eleven. 11 - 6 = 5 cards out higher than the 6. Dummy's 2 + his 2 leaves the declarer with 1 winner in spades. When South wins the spade, he goes to the board with a diamond and tries to steal 1 heart trick for his ninth trick. East must play "second hand high" in this situation. How does East know South has only 3 spades? HE LISTENED to the bidding – South denied a 4-card major when he bid 2 diamonds after North's 2 club inquiry.

Tip: One of the reasons a declarer in NT counts winners BEFORE beginning the play is to determine where his "contracted" tricks are coming from. Many times a good declarer will go "stealing" early in the play to keep opponents from recognizing his motive. He must get his book before defenders get their book! Think, Listen, Count.

Declarer South 4 Hearts
None Vulnerable

The Defense of the Hand
Showing Attitude, then Suit Preference

North
S K J 10 8
H A J 3
D 9 7 4
C K J 3

West
S 6 3 2
H 10 7 4
D A K
C 9 7 5 4 2

East
S A 9 5 4
H 6
D J 8 6 5 2
C Q 10 8

South (dealer)
S Q 7
H K Q 9 8 5 2
D Q 10 3
C A 6

The Bidding: South 1 heart – West pass – North 3 hearts – East pass – South 4 hearts – West pass, pass, pass.

The Lead: The King of diamonds

The Defense: East plays the 2 of diamonds denying an equal honor in diamonds BUT when West continues with the Ace of diamonds, East realizes his partner holds only 2 diamonds. When East recognizes his partner's motive, he discards the Jack to show partner how he can reach the East hand. West switches to a small spade and trumps East's diamond return with the 7 to begin a **trump echo showing 3 cards in trump suit**.

Tips: When holding only two cards in a suit which you wish to ruff later in the play, play them in inverted order (KA) to get partner's attention.

North's 3-heart bid here is traditional and forcing.

Declarer South 5 clubs
None Vulnerable

The Defense of the Hand
Suit Preference Signals
when Declarer Leads

North
S K J 6 4
H 3
D K J 4 2
C K 10 4 2

West
S 9 7 5 3
H 9 7 5 4
D 10 5 3
C A 6

East (dealer)
S A Q 2
H K Q J 10 8 6 2
D 9 8 7
C --

South
S 10 8
H A
D A Q 6
C Q J 9 8 7 5 3

The Bidding: East 1 heart – South 2 clubs – West pass – North 4 clubs – East 4 hearts – South 5 clubs – West pass, pass, pass.

The Lead: The 4 of hearts, East plays the 10

The Defense: South wins the heart lead and leads a club (trumps) – West wins the Ace. East discards the King of hearts – a signal for a spade lead. The contract is defeated – Good defense!

Tip: An unusually high discard asks partner to switch suits on his next lead. As it is on this hand, it must be obvious to both partners that it isn't an attitude signal.

Declarer South 4 Hearts
None Vulnerable

The Defense of the Hand
Suit Preference Signals
to Show Partner an Entry

North
S Q 7 2
H K J 9 5
D K 6 3
C K Q 7

West
S 8
H 7 4 2
D J 10 9
C 9 8 6 5 4 2

East
S A J 9 6 4 3
H --
D Q 8 4 2
C A 10 3

South (dealer)
S K 10 5
H A Q 10 8 6 3
D A 7 5
C J

The Bidding: South 1 heart – West pass – North 3 hearts – East 3 spades – South 4 hearts – West pass, pass, pass.

The Lead: The 8 of spades

The Defense: East wins the Ace of spades and returns the 3 to request a club return (the lowest ranked of 2 remaining suits). West trumps with the 4 to begin the Trump Echo showing a 3-card holding in the trump suit. West trumps the second spade return and plays the Jack of diamonds – a safe lead – his work is "done".

Tip: When leading a singleton which is won by partner, the size of partner's card returned shows suit preference; if it is a small card, he is requesting the return of the lower-ranked suit (never trumps). If it is **above a 6**, he is requesting the return of the higher-ranked suit.

212

Declarer South 4 Spades
None Vulnerable

The Defense of the Hand
Attitude Signals
at Suit Contracts

North
S J 10 7 3
H 6 2
D A Q J 10
C K J 4

West
S 8 2
H A K J 10 7 4
D 9 6 5 3
C 5

East
S Q 5
H 9 8
D K 7 4
C Q 10 8 6 3 2

South (dealer)
S A K 9 6 4
H Q 5 3
D 8 2
C A 9 7

The Bidding: South 1 spade – West 2 hearts – North 3 spades – East pass – South 4 spades – West pass, pass, pass.

The Lead: The Ace of hearts

The Defense: East follows partner's lead with the 9 then the 8, a high-low to direct his partner to continue with the third heart; he can overruff dummy.

Tips: An attitude signal says, "I like or I don't like your lead." It does not necessarily show strength or weakness. High or high-low, I like; low or low-high, I don't like.

The attitude signal applies when following to a suit led by your partner (you are third hand) AND when discarding. It does not apply when declarer is leading. Partner must take notice of other cards in the suit to determine if the card is low or high on the first lead.

Declarer South 3 NT
None Vulnerable

The Defense of the Hand
Attitude Signals
at Suit Contracts

North (dealer)
S A Q J
H 3 2
D K Q J 8 4
C 6 3 2

West
S 9 5 3
H K Q 10 6 5
D A 6
C 8 7 4

East
S 10 7 6 4 2
H 9 8 7
D 5
C A 10 9 5

South
S K 8
H A J 4
D 10 9 7 3 2
C K Q J

The Bidding: North 1 diamond – East pass – South 2 NT – West pass – North 3 NT – East pass, pass, pass.

The Lead: The King of hearts – which holds

The Defense: West considers that the 7 is the lowest card East holds. He switches to a small club hoping East has the Ace and can lead through declarer's AJ. This enables West to establish his heart suit which, along with the Ace of diamonds, will defeat the contract.

Tips: Attitude signals against a notrump contract are a little more involved than in suit contracts – especially when declarer is running a long suit. If possible, each partner should give a high card from the suit he is protecting on the first discard.

If you don't have a high card you can afford to discard, discard **very low** from suits you **cannot protect**.

214

Declarer South 4 Spades
None Vulnerable

The Defense of the Hand
Count Signals in the Trump Suit

North
S J 8 4
H 7 6 4 2
D Q 9 8 7 5
C A

West
S 7 6 2
H Q J 10 5 3
D 3
C J 9 8 4

East
S A 5
H K 9 8
D A 6 4 2
C 7 5 3 2

South (dealer)
S K Q 10 9 3
H A
D K J 10
C K Q 10 6

The Bidding: South 1 spade – West pass – North 2 spades – East pass – South 4 spades – West pass, pass, pass.

The Lead: The 3 of diamonds

The Defense: East wins the Ace of diamonds and returns the 6 asking partner to lead a heart. West ruffs with the 6 and returns the Queen of hearts (since he holds a sequence). Declarer wins the heart lead and plays the King of spades, West plays the **2 to complete the trump echo**. When East wins the Ace of trumps, he gives partner another ruff. Poor opponents – they are down one thanks to the Trump Echo.

Tip: Giving trump count is the opposite of giving count in all other suits.
Play middle-low with an odd number – play low-high with an even number.

Declarer South 4 Spades
None Vulnerable

The Defense of the Hand
Count Signals in the Trump Suit

North (dealer)
S A 9 8 3
H K Q 5
D A Q J 10
C K 6

West
S K J
H 10 9 8 7 6
D 5 2
C Q J 4 3

East
S 5 4
H A 2
D 8 6 4 3
C A 10 9 8 5

South
S Q 10 7 6 2
H J 4 3
D K 9 7
C 7 2

The Bidding: North 1 diamond – East pass – South 1 spade – West pass – North 4 spades – East pass, pass, pass.

The Lead: The 10 of hearts

The Defense: East wins the Ace of hearts and returns the 2, declarer wins and leads a trump – East playing the 4. West wins the second spade lead – BUT – partner plays the 5 showing an **even** number of trumps. That party is over! West now leads the Queen of clubs.

A REVIEW
TERMS AND NUMBERS TO REMEMBER

• Simple bid	A non-jump call
• LMR (Limit Major Raise)	10-11
• Reverse bid	17
• Jump, same suit (opener)	17
• Jump shift, NT	18
• Jump shift, suit	19-21
• Strong 2 Club Artificial Opening	22
• 1 NT opening	15-17
• 2 NT opening	20-21
• Stayman	Got a 4-card major?
• Jacoby Transfer	The big hand declares
• Small slam	33
• Grand slam	37
• Blackwood	Suit contracts
• Gerber	Notrump contracts
• Splinters	Double Jump Bid 13-16 points
• Jacoby 2 NT	13+ HCP's – no upward limit
• Competing after NT	Cappelletti
• Grand Slam Force	5 NT
• Roman Key Card Blackwood	Specific controls
• Western Cue Bid	Got a stopper?
• Two-Suited Overcalls	
○ Unusual Notrump	For the minors
○ Michaels Cue Bid	For the majors
• Preempts	
○ 3 Level and above	7+ cards
○ Weak-Twos	6 cards

ADDITIONAL POPULAR CONVENTIONS

Bergen Major Suit Raises

Bergen Major Suit Raises devised by Mr. Marty Bergen, an outstanding player and author, is a series of responses to a one-level major suit opening. They are preemptive measures as well as very descriptive of responder's hand value. The theory behind them as related in Mr. Larry Cohen's **The Law of Total Tricks**, is that the total number of trumps held by a partnership should strongly relate to the level of a contract.

- A simple raise (1 H/S ↔ 2 H/S) shows 6-9 points and **exactly** 3-card support.
- A jump to 3 H/S (1 H/S ↔ 3 H/S) shows 0-6 points and 4+ card support.
- A jump to 3 clubs (1 H/S ↔ 3 clubs) shows 7-10 points and 4+ card support.
- A jump to 3 diamonds (1 H/S ↔ 3 diamonds) shows 11-12 points and 4+ card support.
- A jump to the 3 level in the other major (1 S ↔ 3 H or 1 H ↔ 3 S) shows 13+ points, and a side suit singleton or void in an unspecified suit. The opener bids the next available suit to find the shortness:
  - 1 S ↔ 3 H ↔ 3 S (the next available suit) or
  - 1 H ↔ 3 S ↔ 4 clubs
- A jump to 3 NT (1 H/S ↔ 3 NT) shows a balanced hand, 13+ points, all suits stopped and **exactly** 3-card support.
  - The opener places the final contract.
- A jump to 4 H/S is bid traditionally, i.e, 0-7 HCP's (1 H/S ↔ 4 H/S), 5+ cards, usually with a singleton or a void and one outside Ace.

The above responses are artificial and forcing except the simple raise and perhaps the 3 NT call. All responses should be alerted. Discuss with partners whether interference changes the meanings of the responses.

If this convention is adopted, 3 diamonds can substitute for a limit major raise if 11-12 is your pointcount range. The system doesn't conflict with Jacoby 2 NT, splinter bids, Jordan 2 NT nor Grand Slam Force.

Summary Responses
Bergen Opening 1 H/S

- 2 H/S   ↔   6-9 points   ↔   3 cards
- 3 H/S   ↔   0-6 points   ↔   4+ cards
- 3 clubs   ↔   7-10 points   ↔   4+ cards
- 3 diamonds   ↔   11-12 points   ↔   4+ cards
- 3 of other major shows a singleton   ↔   4+ cards
- 3 NT   ↔   13+ balanced points   ↔   3 cards
- 4 H/S   ↔   0-7 points   ↔   5+ cards

Brozel

Brozel is another convention used to compete for the contract after **opponent opens 1 NT**:

- Double shows a one-suited hand. Partner bids two clubs. The doubler bids his suit.

- Two clubs shows clubs and hearts.

- Two diamonds shows diamonds and hearts.

- Two hearts shows hearts and spades.

- Two spades shows spades and an unspecified minor. Partner bids 2 NT to find which minor.

- 2 NT shows clubs and diamonds.

- 3 C/D/H/S shows a strong suit and game-going values.

If using Brozel, the double of 1 NT cannot be used as a penalty double.

DONT

DONT (Disturb Opponents NT) may be used to compete for the contract

after **opponent opens 1 NT as follows:**

- Double shows a one-suited hand of either hearts, diamonds or clubs. Responder bids 2 NT to find the suit.

- Two clubs shows clubs and another suit. Responder bids 2 NT to find the other suit.

- Two diamonds shows diamonds and a major suit. Responder bids 2 NT to find the major.

- Two hearts shows hearts and spades. Responder bids his best of the two suits.

- Two spades shows spades.

If this convention is used, the double of 1 NT cannot be used for penalty.

Flannery 2 Diamonds

Flannery 2 Diamonds is an opening call which is preemptive and descriptive.

The 2 diamond bidder holds exactly **4 spades and 5 hearts**. His

pointcount is **11-15**. This is used as a replacement for the weak two diamond

bid but does not affect other weak two calls.

Responder Bids
- 2 hearts or 2 spades, a sign-off
- 3 hearts or 3 spades, invitational
- 3 NT, 4 hearts or 4 spades, a sign-off
- A 2 NT response to Flannery asks opener to further describe his hand shown following:

Opener	Responder	Opener's Rebids
2 diamonds	2 NT	

- 3 C/D shows 3 cards in that suit (thus a singleton in the other minor (4 + 5 + 3 = 12).

- 3 hearts shows 11-13 points, 2 cards in each minor.

- 3 spades shows 14-15 points, 2 cards in each minor.

- 3 NT shows 14-15 points with a protected honor in each minor.

- 4 clubs or diamonds shows 4 of that suit and thus a void in the other suit.

All of the opener's rebids are artificial and forcing. The responder places the final contract.

New Minor Forcing

New Minor Forcing is used when partner opens one of a minor and rebids 1 NT after a major suit response. A bid of the other minor ("new") asks partner if he has 3-card support for your **5 card suit**. This keeps the bidding lower than a rebid. (Partner 1 diamond – You 1 spade – Partner 1 NT – You **2 clubs**, a new minor.) Opener raises with 3 cards or makes another call with less than 3.

Ogust

Ogust is a 2 NT response to partner's weak two opening. It asks opener to describe the **strength** of his **suit** and the relative **strength** of his **hand**.

Opener	Responder
2 D/H/S	2 NT

Opener's Rebid

• 3 clubs	↔	weak suit	↔	Minimum strength
• 3 diamonds	↔	good suit	↔	Minimum strength
• 3 hearts	↔	weak suit	↔	Maximum strength
• 3 spades	↔	good suit	↔	Maximum strength

One Notrump Forcing

One Notrump Forcing after a 1 H/S opening is an integral component in the two over one system; but, it may also be used with Standard American bidding. Its purpose is to allow opener and responder to more narrowly define hand value. It **shows 6-12 points** and is forcing one round.

Opener	Responder	Opener's Rebids
1 H/S	1 NT (forcing)	• A rebid of same suit shows a minimum of 6 cards.
		• A 3-club or 3-diamond response shows 3+ cards (with both, bid clubs).
		• A bid of hearts after a spade opening shows a minimum of 4 cards.
		• A raise of 1 NT shows 18+ HCP's and balanced distribution.

Responder's Rebids

- With 2/3-card support ↔ 6-9 points ↔ a simple raise

- With 3-card support ↔ 10-11 points ↔ a jump raise

- With 4-card support, non-vulnerable against vulnerable opponents, preempt to game level.

- A simple rebid of a new suit shows 5+ cards and is non - forcing.

The Responsive Double

The Responsive Double is an extension of the takeout double. Its purpose is to locate the longest suit for trumps. The context is which it is used is as follows:

When partner has doubled opponent 1 for takeout AND opponent 2 **raises** the suit his partner opened, fourth hand may use the responsive double to show values without length. Second hand chooses the trump suit.

The Bidding

(1)

Opponent 1	Partner	Opponent 2	You
1 diamond	double	2 diamonds	double
Your hand:			S 10 9 8 6
			H A J 9 4
			D K 5
			C J 10 9

You have equal length in both majors.

(2)

Opponent 1	Partner	Opponent 2	You
1 club	double	3 clubs	3 hearts
Your hand:			S A J 10 4
			H Q J 6 5 4
			D Q 4
			C 5 4

You have 5 hearts, so bid them!

When one major has been bid, the responsive double tends to show both minors. (If your partner has 5 cards in the other major, he will have overcalled that suit. If he has only 4, he will show them after you have used the responsive double.)

(3)	Opponent 1	Partner	Opponent 2	You
	1 heart	double	2 hearts	• double
	pass	2 spades		• raise OR bid longest minor

Your hand:

S 10 9 8
H A 6
D K J 10 9 8
C Q J 9

Your bid:
Partner pass

3 diamonds

Summary
The Responsive Double

- 6 HCP's   ↔   2 level
- 8 HCP's   ↔   3 level
- 10 HCP's   ↔   4 level

Bidding after Responsive Double

- Minimum bid   ↔   minimum value
- Jump bid   ↔   extra values
- NT bid   ↔   stoppers in opponents' suit
- Cue bid of opponents' suit   ↔   game force

Responsive Doubles after Partner Overcalls:

Opponent 1	Partner	Opponent 2	You
1 heart	1 spade	2 hearts	double

Your double shows values in the minor suits.

IMPORTANT

Do not use the responsive double unless opponents have agreed on a suit.

Reverse Drury Convention

Reverse Drury is a response of 2 clubs after partner opens 1 H/S in third or fourth position which is often light in HCP's. It asks partner if he has a full opening hand. Opener responds as follows:

- 2 **diamonds** shows a **full** opening hand.
- 2 of the **same suit denies** a full opening (Doesn't necessarily show over 5 cards.)
- 2 **hearts** after a 1 spade opening shows 4+cards and **denies** a full opening.

The 2-diamond bid is artificial and forcing unless there is an intervening bid. It is the only call that shows a full opening. Two diamonds originally denied a full opening – thus "Reverse Drury."

Responder rebids as follows:

- Two of the major shows 11 points – not forcing.
- Any other rebid is natural and shows support for partner's major.
- Three clubs, rebid, shows a real club suit, game-going values. Invitational.
- Three of the major shows game forcing values.

Two NT Response to a Minor Suit Opening

Two NT Response to a Minor Suit Opening shows 11-12 points and is non-forcing/invitational. When using this convention, one notrump shows 6-9(10) and 3 NT shows 13-15 balanced points. All calls deny a 4-card major.

Weak Jump Shift

A Weak Jump Shift after partner's one level opening bid shows **5 HCP's or less** and 6+cards. Partner will usually pass. Its purpose is to preempt opponents and announce to partner the holding of a weak hand with a long suit. You will recall responder does NOT jump shift on his first call in standard bidding.